gil rendle

D1509196

the multigenerational congregation

meeting the leadership challenge

foreword by lovett h. weems, jr.

an alban institute publication

The writing of this book was supported by a generous grant from the Louisville Institute, a Lilly Endowment Program for the Study of American Religion based at Louisville Seminary, Louisville, Kentucky.

Library of Congress Card Number 2001094869
ISBN 1-56699-252-4

10   09   08   07   06   05   WP   2   3   4   5   6   7   8   9

CONTENTS

"It is no easy task to build up the faith of one generation, and not destroy the supports of the religion of the other," wrote a young Detroit pastor named Reinhold Niebuhr in 1921.

Gil Rendle has captured the dilemma faced by countless clergy seeking to lead within congregations made up of persons who, while liking each other, simply see the world in fundamentally different ways. While many authors have contributed significantly to our understanding of key generational cohorts, Rendle takes a different approach in *The Multigenerational Congregation*. While drawing from generational literature, Rendle acknowledges a key limitation to its implementation within local churches.

Local churches are almost never what the advertising world calls "pure markets" made up of only one generational constituency. Effective church leaders have to contend with the worldviews of multiple generations. These "bi-modal congregations" contain at least two different and often competing generational groupings.

Often pastors work diligently to understand the needs of a new generation, implement ways of worship to meet those needs, and succeed in reaching more people, only to be criticized by congregational leaders. Hence the need to understand that church leadership in the multigenerational congregation requires more than understanding the preferences of the different generational constituencies within the church. Such leadership requires finding new ways to address the real generational differences that are present.

The multigenerational congregation presents a challenge but not a problem. Such a congregation is actually a healthy congregation, while uncomfortable for the leader. Rendle reminds us that it is such congregations that are receiving new members, passing on the faith to new generations, and are having an earnest dialogue about what is truly important. Health does not make leadership any easier, but it puts the challenge in proper perspective. This healthy tension is a sign of life and hope for the future.

Rendle does a marvelous job of outlining an interactive approach to leadership that refuses neither to adapt to the most comfortable option of inaction nor to introduce change in a manner that disrupts the very Christian community of faith that is ultimately sought. His suggestions are to move to the balcony and get the larger picture, speak descriptively rather than evaluatively, seek common space for people with differences, and practice civility.

Religious leaders can learn much from the lessons related to the multigenerational congregation. In fact, the challenge of such churches is the challenge of our society. The challenge of creating community within the differences of congregations is the task of our world today. Churches that are "impure markets in a pure market world" help remind a world focused on differences that true community finds unity while honoring differences. Such leadership is not always neat and predictable. It means a leader will at times be the voice of continuity and at other times, the voice of change. In some situations the leader is the most conserving force and in other situations, the most liberating.

Religious leaders by definition are people with strong beliefs and values. Yet the challenge for effective church leaders is to find a way to lead God's people in discovering what is needed for faithfulness in a particular place and time. Leaders always work in the midst of competing values. Rendle reminds us that the competition is not just between a leader's values and those of a congregation. The congregation itself often bears multiple traditions and values.

The multigenerational congregation requires leaders who take seriously their own values and the multiple values found within their context. To ask the question, "Which way should I lean in this situation?" is not a surrender of one's personal integrity. Integrity does not mean doing and saying the same thing in every situation. While remaining consistent in overall values and goals, leaders understand that different occasions call for different responses. The key questions revolve around what is most needed in the present situation. The goal remains to help a particular community of faith take their next faithful step toward the worshipping and serving church God calls them to be.

What then about legitimate and deeply held differences? They remain. But no longer are these differences the ways that we define ourselves within a congregation. Rather we define ourselves in terms of what we have in common—the Christ who is at the center. Once we no longer define ourselves strictly by our generational or other categories, we are in a better position to deal with the differences that are there.

Without a unifying vision centered in Christ that captures the imagination of everyone, our differences simply become more dominant. When there is central unity, the differences remain but are put in perspective. What was once a liability now becomes an expression of the richness of our church from which to draw God's wisdom and gifts so amply represented in all.

Leaders in multigenerational congregations need neither to fear nor glamorize conflict and differences. They understand that a degree of tension accompanies growth and maturity. Rendle reminds such leaders that their task is neither to resolve the tension through victory for one side over the other, nor through compromise that destroys the richness of the different perspectives. God's leaders trust that out of healthy dialogue and discernment, God will indeed do a "new thing" that far surpasses any premature solution even the wisest leader might have conceived.

LOVETT H. WEEMS, JR.

Have you ever been the leader in a situation that you couldn't win, no matter which way you went? Say, for example, you are responsible for training and supervising the acolytes at your church. The older members pull you aside to point out that the teenagers who light the candles don't dress appropriately. You regularly field complaints about the sneakers and jeans glaringly visible beneath the acolyte gowns. You talk to the teens, who assure you that they *are* wearing their "good" clothes to church. They also let you know that they are not interested in "acolyting" if they have to wear "dress shoes." Your conversations with the parents don't help: They are pleased just to get their teens to attend worship, however they are dressed.

This small drama is played out in many congregations. It is not unimportant to the people involved. I once joked to some adults that they seemed to believe that if the altar candles were lit by a sneaker-clad adolescent, they weren't truly lit, and worship could not begin. The joke was on me: My listeners didn't think my comment was at all funny and, yes, it was much harder for them to worship with sneakered acolytes.

What does the leader do? Live with unanswered complaints about sneakers? Insist on dress shoes and then explain to the worship committee why you can't recruit enough teens, especially boys, to serve as acolytes? Put pressure on the parents, who are already harried by this struggle and don't want to deal with it anymore? Suffer the stress in silence and do what your predecessor did—get off the worship committee at the first opportunity?

Such disagreements in congregations are neither unimportant nor inconsequential. In fact, they are part of a valuable discourse. These conversations often divide along generational lines; the subtext is an inquiry into what is important to our worship and faith practice from the perspectives and preferences of different generations. The discourse often centers on what is to be preserved, changed, jettisoned, or disallowed in this time of rapid change. As a congregational consultant, I am one of a host of people who have the privilege and pain of visiting congregations that are engaged in these conversations about what is important.

Keepers and Shapers of the Tradition

People attempting to cope with a quickly changing environment need institutions that can respond sensitively. It is widely understood that congregations are keepers of long and valued traditions of faith and culture. As keepers of tradition, congregants are not simply individuals entrenched in their preferred habits. A deeper concern is also at issue. As Sidney Schwarz, president of the Washington Institute for Jewish Leadership and Values, notes:

> Religion is highly resistant to change. As it passes traditions from one generation to the next, rituals, ceremonies, and religious text represent a tie to the past, a connection to a transcendent history. Peter Berger, in his classic work *The Sacred Canopy*, observes that as churches seek to keep pace with changes in the cultural context in which they find themselves, they put at risk the "plausibility" that confers upon them the legitimacy in the eyes of adherents. That plausibility is tied to the ability of a religious system to embody an ancient tradition.[1]

Schwarz goes on to say, "It is thus no easy task to create major change in synagogues that are the retail outlets through which most Jews experience Judaism." And it is no easier to create major change in Protestant or Catholic congregations. Nonetheless, these congregations need to respond in new ways to the changes that are shaping the people they seek to serve. Congregations need to learn new cultural languages and practices to speak to and to be heard by new generations.

Yet in many long-established congregations, cultural changes are commonly resisted, and new ways of speaking about and sharing faith are challenged rather than embraced. Traditions and practices that strengthened and supported one generation are held tightly rather than being adjusted or replaced to strengthen and support faith in the next generations.

Key leaders in congregations spend their time and energy trying to understand cultural shifts and the needs of new generations, only to be resisted or opposed by the generations well established in the congregation.

Rather than finding appreciation for experimental practices that might speak to new generations seeking faith, leaders not uncommonly discover that such experiments can easily become the evidence used against them when members of the established generations challenge their leadership.

While dangerously amusing, the experience of one midsize congregation is not unusual in its members' confrontation of their pastor with his "betrayal." The congregation was located in a small county-seat town surrounded by a long-established rural county where farm families could trace their histories back for several generations. But because of the presence of the county courthouse and the surrounding support offices and businesses, the town was growing and changing with an influx of new, younger residents who had no previous roots in the area. The new neighbors began to attend worship at this congregation with some enthusiasm, responding to the ministry of the pastor and a few key lay leaders who had done their homework and understood the needs and changes sought by the new arrivals.

Sides were drawn and the battle was openly engaged when the pastor included drums and guitars in the new alternative worship service established for the newcomers. The new service offered an added worship setting for the congregation, while the traditional service retained its customary time and liturgy. Nonetheless, the pastor received complaints from long-tenured members. Faced with their gripes, the pastor quickly sought a compromise. He pointed out that the complaining members weren't required to attend the new service; they could continue to attend the regular, unchanged worship service at the usual hour. The opponents countered that they couldn't worship in the regular service if they couldn't avoid the sight of the large drum set, which had been placed in the chancel area next to the organ. Again seeking compromise, the pastor covered the drums with a drape that was congruent with the altar-area paraments. But the complaints continued: Long-term members stated firmly that they couldn't worship knowing what was *under* the drape. Still committed to compromise, the pastor moved the alternative service to the adjoining Sunday school auditorium—which, in this congregation's facility, was adjacent to, but visible from, the sanctuary. Unfortunately, the large movable partitions, originally designed to separate the building's two sections, had long ago stopped functioning.

Reasoning that he had responded sufficiently by removing the offending musical instruments and taking the alternative service out of the established worship space, the pastor asked the governing board to call a consultant to work with the congregation. By now, he was being attacked by complainers growing even angrier with their pastor because they could "still see those damned drums over there in the other room!"

Across the American religious landscape such experiments designed to speak to and include new generations are similarly resisted and challenged. That the landscape of new generations is changing is not in dispute. People inside and outside congregations are well aware of the cultural changes we share as we are being changed by a media- and technology-driven information age. That congregations need to wrestle with the changes and find a way to address them is also not in dispute. Leaders in the most resistant congregations are regularly urged by their members and boards to "do something" to bring in new members. Members may give the pastor a mandate to lead the congregation into the wilderness of ministry with new generations, but that does not mean that long-time congregants will enjoy the trip.

Congregations—Protestant, Catholic, and Jewish—*are increasingly structured for just this kind of internal discomfort and debate.* The Alban Institute's experience and consultations with congregations of multiple faith traditions and denominations across the United States and Canada have helped to developed a growing awareness of a change in the internal structure of many of our congregations.

I call this new shape the "bimodal" congregation, a singularly unattractive but descriptive term indicating that our congregations are increasingly housing populations with at least two centers of influence, often in competition. Many congregations have a large cluster of longtime active members. These same congregations increasingly have a similarly large, or even larger, cluster of members and participants who have been active in the congregation for only a short time. Finally, it is quite common that these congregations have a very small cluster of members in the middle who have been in the congregation for a mid-length period. This dearth of mid-length members is often referred to in the conversations of these congregations as their "missing generation."

The large clusters of long-tenured members and short-tenured members are commonly experienced as competing centers of influence in the life of the congregation. This tension between groups is often referred to as "the old guard vs. the new guard." However, the relationship need not be an oppositional state dividing two groups of people who, in fact, most often truly like and want to be with one another. In fact, the conversation between longer-tenured and shorter-tenured members is critical theological discourse that needs to be understood, protected, and shaped by the congregation's leaders.

This tension between the competing centers of influence does not have to be cast as a problem. In fact, to approach these conversations as a problem is to assume that an identifiable solution exists. To "solve" many of the debates is to declare a winner and, by default, a loser. Such problem-solving responses divide the congregation more sharply. Too often our search for solutions brings to a halt prematurely a dynamic, productive, and necessary conversation about how we can shape and shift our faith traditions to help people of faith live with vibrancy in a developing new world, while keeping their truths intact.

Elsewhere I have written and spoken about the need for current leaders, lay and clergy, to develop more than problem-solving skills and assumptions to provide the leadership needed by congregations today.[2] One of my favorite bromides says, "If the only thing you have is a hammer, everything you see looks like a nail." Similarly, if the only available tool that leaders have is the basic problem-solving process that most of us employ, then the only way they can view discomfort is as a problem. A critical challenge congregational leaders face is the need to preserve and protect the discomfort of differences among the people as an opportunity for learning rather than to seek quick solutions that will make winners comfortable and cause losers to disappear.

A Healthy, but Uncomfortable Congregation

The critical point is that the bimodal congregation pictured in this book is a *healthy congregation*, though not necessarily always a *comfortable* congregation. It is not necessarily a congregation that is always easy on its leaders. But it is a healthy congregation that:

- *Is receiving new members.* This bimodal congregation would not be uncomfortable if it did not have the ability to call and receive from the culture new members who come with new ideas and expectations.

Healthy systems have interdependent relationships with their environment, and they have porous boundaries through which one can move in
and out. The bimodal congregation, with its discomfort, is evidence that
when you open the doors, new people will come in. The bimodal congregation is in a healthy relationship with its environment.

- *Is passing on the faith.* While, surprisingly, it seems that the *length* of
  one's membership in a congregation is the stronger determinant of one's
  behavior and preferences, there is obviously a *generational* corollary
  to what I describe here. The bimodal congregation is a primary platform from which one generation passes the truth, the disciplines, and
  the traditions of a faith to another generation. In fact, it can be argued
  that unless congregations learn to manage the current generational differences and expectations, they will have to struggle even harder to
  pass on the faith to the generational cohorts that are beginning to line
  up behind those now in the congregation.

- *Is in earnest dialogue about what's important.* Do not dismiss as
  insignificant the story about the sneakers and the candles. Yes, what
  people wear to worship is to a great degree a matter of preference.
  But the argument goes much deeper as people debate the presence
  and meaning of sacred symbols. In this case there is an argument over
  which symbols are sacred. Are the lit candles sacred symbols signify-
  ing the appropriate environment for worship and connection with God?
  If so, the candles can be lit by people wearing any kind of footwear. Or
  is it the more formal dress and attention to manner and demeanor that
  mark the place and time of Sabbath as sacred and different from common days? If this is the case, the shoes and demeanor of those lighting
  the candles have a sacred aspect as well. This is, in fact, an important
  conversation for a healthy congregation. That it comes out as debate
  or argument is evidence of life and health. "When a tradition is 'living,'" writes Dorothy Bass, professor of theology at Valparaiso University, in Indiana, "its members are engaged in a vibrant, embodied
  'argument,' stretching across time and space, about what the fullest
  participation in its particular goods would entail."[3]

The point that the tensions in the bimodal congregation can be evidence of health does not make the congregation any easier to lead. Perhaps, for the moment, the bimodal makeup of many congregations is a
snapshot of a step in the progress toward the "once and future church."

CHRISTIAN
REFORMED
CHURCH

July 2007

Dear Kevin,

These books are for the Pastor of Larger Churches peer group gathering coming up this fall. We will be paying particular attention to the *Multigenerational Congregation* book at the fall session. More details will be shared in the coming month as to how this looks as part of your preparation for our gathering.

Thank you and we look forward to seeing you in the fall!

In writing about the transition from the Christendom paradigm to a new, not-yet-formed, post-Christendom paradigm, Loren Mead says, "I do not expect clarity about the new church for several generations—I shall not see it, even though I work for it. That lack of clarity is true for most of us, I think."[4] We are reminded that we may well be looking at evidence of how our congregations are managing the transition into the new world, the new paradigm. The behavior of the bimodal congregation, I would suggest, offers more to instruct us and to help us than we might have thought. After all, the tensions within the bimodal congregation are driven largely by generational differences that leaders must learn how to negotiate if the congregants are to move with confidence into the future.

We are also reminded that we have not yet reached the destination in this transition that is not only generational but also global and cultural. As ample as the evidence may be that we are well on our way to post-Christendom and postmodern health, we are still assuredly not further along than the uncomfortable middle stage of transition. William Bridges, consultant and lecturer on managing transition, calls this middle phase the "neutral zone," the time between letting go of our old ways of "doing" faith" and the claiming of new beginnings in which we feel assured that we know where to go:

> If this phase lasted only a short time, you could just wait for it to pass. But when the change is deep and far-reaching, this time between the old identity and the new can stretch out for months, even years. This, as Marilyn Ferguson [American futurist] says, is a time when you've let go of one trapeze with the faith that the new trapeze is on its way. In the meantime, there's nothing to hold on to.[5]

It is not an easy time to be a congregational leader. A favorite biblical parallel of mine is the image of Moses leading the Israelites into the wilderness to escape slavery. Everybody knew that the trip was important—even lifesaving. The Israelites cheered Moses when they started the trip and when he led them through the Red Sea to escape their captors. Nonetheless, we are told in Exodus 16 that only 45 days into the 40-year journey the "people complained against Moses."

> The whole congregation of the Israelites set out from Elim; and Israel came to the wilderness of Sin, which is between Elim and

Sinai, on the fifteenth day of the second month after they had
departed from the land of Egypt. The whole congregation of the
Israelites complained against Moses and Aaron in the wilderness.
The Israelites said to them, "If only we had died by the hand of
the Lord in the land of Egypt, when we sat by the fleshpots and
ate our fill of bread; for you have brought us out into this wilderness to kill this whole assembly with hunger."

Exodus 16:1-3

It seems that one reality for leaders in many congregations caught in the
journey between competing generations, between short- and long-tenured
members, is that leadership is simultaneously demanded and complained
of—often by the same people. If the Israelites complained against Moses
(and Aaron) amid such a lifesaving, indeed people-saving, trip into the wilderness, is it any surprise that leading today's bimodal congregation is often
marked by complaints against leaders who are in fact doing the right and
responsible thing? Perhaps a current mark of effective leaders is that their
people complain about the very effects that come from helping the people
engage and learn about their faith and faith community by exploring their
differences. Is this phenomenon not healthier than complaints in dying congregations where leaders are too timid to enter the wilderness where God is
transforming the people?

What This Book Will Do

A central task of leaders is to pick and shape the kinds of conversation that
others will have with us. Leaders exercise tremendous power and faithfulness by helping others engage in healthy conversations in which people
learn new ideas and skills that will help to build community in our congregations. For example, in board and committee meetings this power of leadership is exercised through the development of the agenda, as the leader says
to the group: In the time available in this meeting it is better that we talk
about this topic rather than that one. The leader uses the agenda to help the
group talk about the important issues facing them. But in other settings and
gatherings, many of which do not involve decision making, leaders need to
help people talk in healthy ways about important things and common things.
This book is intended as a contribution to this conversational task of leaders.

People in congregations experience discomfort and anxiety over the differences and preferences that they encounter. Our members and participants need healthy ways to think about and understand these differences and preferences. They need help in working with each other in creative ways that exceed the limits of efforts to persuade one another that lead to winning and losing. This book is a tool for leaders to turn painful and destructive conversation about differences into healthier conversations about life in a faith community.

To support and provide resources for healthier understandings and conversations, this book describes what is normative and normal in our often-uncomfortable congregations. A proverb attributed to a Chinese source says, "The beginning of wisdom is to call things by their right name." This book is an effort to call difficult experiences in our congregations by their right names, so that our leaders can see that arguments are normal and, indeed, necessary. A leader's inability to see the normal and normative most often leads to blame as people go in search of an answer to the question, "*Who caused* this discomfort or problem?" This inability also makes for bruised or injured leaders as they too quickly take personally the criticism that belongs to the natural engagement in our increasingly diverse congregations.

We need new ways to think about the generational differences in our congregations. Much of the current literature on generations available to congregational leaders reifies the differences, drawing clear lines between the GI generation and the baby boomers, between early boomers and late boomers, between boomers and busters, between moderns and postmoderns; and distinguishes among a host of other generational and experiential markers established by an advertising- and media-driven culture. This information is helpful to a point. But the overwhelming majority of our congregations are not made up of only one of these generational or cultural subgroups—a necessary configuration if we were to do ministry with one group as though it were the sole object. Ministry is much messier that that. We must try to imagine how to do boomer ministry with GIs looking over our shoulders, or GenX ministry with a worship committee filled with boomers who are more comfortable calling these younger folk "slackers."

In other words, we need to learn how to do ministry with one group while other groups are looking on critically, telling us we are doing it wrong. One noteworthy lesson to heed in generational-cohort theory is that generations routinely speak badly of one another because of their differences.

Such criticism is understandable, given that the values shaped and carried by each new generational cohort are meant to offer correction and balance to the limitations and restrictions perceived in the normative practices and principles of the preceding generation.[6] Although speaking ill of the norms and assumptions of others may be a natural place to begin conversation, this book is an effort to help people in congregations move past this limited reality to find the sense of community we seek as people of faith.

I invite you to consider, as you read this book, the ways in which you might engage others in conversation about your reading and how it applies to your congregation. The ideas here concern how and why people with generational differences need to live side by side in congregations. I will offer ideas of how our congregations are structured to experience discomfort over these differences and explain why that discomfort is valuable. You will read stories and examples of other congregations that share in this normal and valuable time of discomfort. The ideas, tools, and strategies in this book are designed to help you deal with these tensions. Perhaps most important, the ideas, stories, and biblical texts in this book suggest that leadership in this congregational setting is a spiritual responsibility—a spiritual act that can take us much deeper than efficient organizational management or effective congregational growth.

I encourage you, as you read this book, to ask yourself who should be talking about this topic and how you will lead them to talk about it. If one of the central tasks of leadership is to shape a healthy conversation that leads people to new learning and new faithfulness, who needs to be a part of this conversation in your congregation, and how will you invite them into it? If the beginning of wisdom is to call things by their right name, whom will you invite to join you in learning these new names, so that you can step beyond the old and limited habits of criticism and blame?

CHAPTER 1

Ministry in an Impure Market

There are a hundred ways to clean a kitchen—unless you're in my mother's kitchen.

Anonymous

The pinch that many congregations experience comes not from an inability to attempt changes that speak to the new culture. A wonderful quantity and variety of experimentation are taking place in congregations that have found ways to invite and engage new cohorts of people in practices of faith and community. The pinch comes when congregational leaders attempt new ways to engage new people while established members are looking over their shoulders telling them they are "doing it wrong."

One pastor was leading an informal and spontaneous contemporary worship service. He and his leadership team had done their homework. The service of worship they had designed was free flowing and spontaneous. The texts of hymns or praise songs were projected on large screen up front, freeing people from holding hymnals. Unconstrained in their movement, worshipers felt encouraged to participate and to offer open responses. The service was theologically open to the movement of the spirit of the people as well as the Spirit of God. The pastor worked diligently with the worship leadership team to embody such principles of worship. The response was gratifying. A new group of people gathered in this congregation, their presence centered on this new form of worship. Most who attended were new to the congregation, many of them also new to the faith, having come with no previous faith practice or congregational experience to shape or guide their way. They were, as a group, much younger than the longer-tenured members who attended in the 8:45 A.M. traditional worship, led by the same pastor but by a different music director.

One Sunday, preaching at the 11 A.M. contemporary service, the minister said something that struck a responsive chord in the music director. The principles of free flow and spontaneity were sufficiently internalized by the worship leaders that the music director immediately began to play a song

that fit the point that the minister had just made, encouraging the congregation into song—unplanned, smack in the middle of the sermon. No one saw
it coming—especially not the minister, who was taken aback and had to
refocus his attention to pick up and continue preaching when the singing
ended.

By Tuesday, a furor had broken out over the musician's "inappropriate" intervention. His musical interruption of the sermon was seen as an
effrontery in worship and highly discourteous to the minister. People talked
about the music director's poor judgment. Members dredged up memories
of other instances when, in their view, the director's behavior had been out
of bounds.

Although the minister was startled by the spontaneous interjection of
music into his sermon, he understood the music director's actions and saw
how the curious behavior fitted appropriately the contemporary worship
setting that the worship leadership team had created. He did tell the music
director that he needed cues when something unplanned was about to happen in worship, so that he would not be taken by surprise. But for the
minister, the issue was resolved; a new understanding had been struck with
the music director. What puzzled the pastor was how he could possibly
respond to the furor erupting within the membership over this incident *since
the people who were upset attended the 8:45 A.M. traditional service
and had not been present for the incident.*

What was going on here? Obviously congregants had different ideas
of what constituted appropriate and vital worship for this congregation.
Clearly the two worship services offered at 8:45 and 11:00 were designed
for different groups of worshipers. Hadn't the minister and worship leaders
succeeded in grasping the opportunity to offer a different style of worship
to attract people in the community who would not otherwise have walked
into their worship space? Then why was the minister besieged with complaints and put in the position of having to defend both himself and the music
director against the fury of people who had not even witnessed the offending incident?

The minister and leadership team had understood the changes they
would have to make to reach a new group of people who would not be
attracted to traditional forms of worship and congregational life. Times had
changed, new generations had grown up, and cultural values and behaviors
were different enough that new forms of old practices were needed to live
in the new time. The dilemma was this: When new practices are introduced

into an established congregation that is accustomed to certain styles of worship and congregational life that have endured for decades, the new practices are likely to be evaluated by old standards—and found wanting.

Many researchers, writers, teachers, and denominational leaders have done extensive studies of our shifting cultural practices to help congregations learn how to talk to new groups of people who reflect cultural changes. I believe, however, that the perspective from which writers report their findings differs from the reality in which congregational leaders read about the research outcomes and move toward putting the findings into practice.

Let me critique a few examples of good work that is meant to help congregations come to terms with the changing culture. Consider Craig Kennet Miller's book on "postmoderns," in which he focuses on the generation born between 1965 and 1981. Miller, director of new congregational development for the Nashville-based General Board of Discipleship of the United Methodist Church, is responsible for helping his denomination organize new churches to speak to the contemporary culture. Miller based his writing on two national surveys of the postmodern generation, consisting of a host of smaller surveys given in high-school classes by teachers, and by volunteers surveying young people in malls. He also supported his findings with multiple personal contacts and interviews. He sought out opportunities to be with and talk to these young people. From his work he culled nine "culture-shift" patterns that need to be understood to connect with this cohort of Americans who tend to find traditional worship and congregational life uninviting:

#1: From Order to Chaos
#2: From the Atom to the Bit
#3: From One Truth to Many Truths
#4: From the War Out There to the War Right Here
#5: From the Traditional Family to the Multifamily
#6: From the Job to the Task
#7: From One Way to Diversity
#8: From Religion to Spirituality
#9: From the Modern to the Postmodern Church[1]

To communicate and do ministry with this cultural group, church leaders need to understand and put into practice their understandings of these culture shifts. *Understanding* must lead to *changes in behaviors* that will evoke a response from the "postmoderns."

For instance, in writing about the shift from the traditional family to the "multifamily," Miller notes that the postmodern generation's experience has been highly influenced by the rigidity of family roles thought to characterize the 1950s and 1960s, and by high divorce rates in their parents' generation. The experience of the postmodern generation supports the unmarried state and single parenthood as common and acceptable lifestyles that may be *chosen.* Congregational leaders must be able to stop picturing young couples' groups as the only or dominant avenue for providing learning and support opportunities for young people joining the congregation. Ministry with these people means providing settings and resources for single parents designed to support their lifestyle as a reasonable "choice" rather than to help them with their "problem." And effective ministry means *not* introducing these new people into established groups of long-term members who assume a "couples culture" and traditional family settings to which the new people do not conform (meaning that the established groups may well find themselves depleted over time as new members opt not to join them).

Congregations must change in substantial ways to respond to today's cultural shifts. Writing in 1996, Leonard Sweet, an academic and entrepreneurial writer on the new culture facing congregations, identified "24 Transitions for the 21st Century Church" as "meta-principles of ministry."[2] Given that these transitions require changes in our behaviors (and how difficult it is for us to change!), 24 meta-principled transitions would appear to require an overwhelming program of change for any congregation that holds to deeply established practices and traditions.

As difficult as managing changes may be, I do not think that this work is the major and most immediate stumbling block that many of our leaders face. Earlier, I suggested that there may be differences between the way writers look at these findings and the way leaders who read about them encounter change in the congregation. The current demographic, generational, cultural, and theological studies are remarkable and helpful. Attention to the multiple groups and subsets of people who come to our congregations has been rich and beneficial. We have been helped to talk to others about our faith and to invite them to join us in exploring their lives of faith and the spirit.

The connection between the new findings about the culture and the process of change in the congregation breaks down when leaders read from this growing body of material and then move directly to implement what they have learned. We often move to put our discoveries into practice as though changes did not need to be negotiated with other cultural sub-groups in the congregations, including members in established leadership positions.

For example, the adult ministries office of United Methodism's Board of Discipleship prepared a summary of the results from a survey administered to 250 congregations identified for their vital ministries with baby boomers (the generation born between 1946 and 1964). The authors explained:

> We surveyed United Methodist Boomers to discern what they are thinking about their faith, religion, and spirituality. In addition, we sought their views about life, world events, and the future. We want to know something about the yearnings of their hearts. *As a result, the General Board of Discipleship seeks to provide resources to meet the faith needs of aging Boomers. It is our desire to help Boomers grow as Christian disciples for the transformation of the world* [emphasis added].[3]

In other words, learning leads to implementations—as a result. While learning should lead to change, this rapid impulse to act invites leaders in congregations to read the material about a subgroup's generational and cultural preferences as if a congregation could attend to those needs separately, and without competition from other subgroups. This insufficient reading of the rich generational and cultural material is encouraged by current marketing and advertising practices. These methods are immeasurably powerful in our lives, though often hidden from direct scrutiny.

Pure-Market Assumptions

If postmoderns are not linear thinkers, if they practice "multitasking" and allow little room in their lives for downtime, silence, or simply sitting, then one might assume that a prayer of confession or a moment of silence in worship would intimidate, confuse, or fail to interest them. The quick response is to move directly to develop new liturgies with action and movement, leaving behind these offending moments of silence. Bill Easum, a consultant to congregations, offers the "five-second test." He suggests that worship leaders make audiotapes of their worship services and listen to a playback with attention to moments of silence. If a silence lasts longer than five seconds (an effect he compares to the discomfort of experiencing dead-air time in a radio broadcast), he advises a revamping of the liturgy to ensure that the worship will speak to postmoderns.[4] Easum's response is directed to the needs of the target audience, the postmoderns; he proposes speaking directly to them, without regard for other audiences or subgroups that may come to worship with other needs or cultural preferences.

It is, in fact, important to know that baby busters and GenX people are action-oriented and will not respond comfortably if the minister is the only worship participant who talks, moves, and assumes an active role. It is quite another issue to move too quickly to introduce clapping, body movement, and multiple worship leaders to a congregation that has a well-established practice that does not include these elements. Yet a reading of the recent literature suggests that the preferences of the busters and GenXers must be met, or the congregation will have no opportunity to do ministry with them. In fact, in the language of marketing experts, our leaders have been falsely encouraged by the current cultural setting to think and act *in "pure market" terms.*

A "pure market" is a developed and discrete subgroup of consumers formed as advertising and media industries determine its specific needs, interests, and preferences. By researching and responding to the unique interests or needs of one cultural subgroup and simultaneously disregarding or offering "negative attention" to other subgroups that don't fit the profile, the advertising industry is able to develop "pure markets" of consumer subgroups. The strategy fits well with the historic American ideal of individualism, taken to extremes in the current cultural moment.

In an insightful study of advertising and the new media, Joseph Turrow, professor in the Annenberg School for Communication at the University of Pennsylvania, documents the search for pure markets and their usefulness in the marketplace.[5] Once, during the Depression and World War II, the American people saw themselves as a group, and the media approached that single America through mass-marketing techniques. In recent decades we have witnessed a remarkable transition: advertisers now pay more attention to our differences, creating smaller and smaller groups within the larger public. Beginning his studies in the 1970s at the time of the initial shift in the marketing industry, Turrow "noticed that media were increasingly encouraging people to separate themselves into more and more specialized groups and to develop distinctive viewing, reading, and listening habits that stressed differences between their groups and others."[6]

As a North American people we have become more sensitive to the differences that divide us than to the common values or preferences that unite us. The gifts of advertising and media have been merged with technology to create an immensely powerful marketing industry capable of finding out our consumer preferences and differences so that marketers can speak to us in "personalized" ways. Using highly technical information systems, multiple databases, and an intricate national marketing strategy that is updated more than 16 million times a day, our individual behaviors and preferences have been tracked through purchasing decisions; billing systems; municipal, state, and federal information sources; and multiple less-formal channels. The media can now provide clear and individualized ways to communicate with us about our lifestyles. For instance, the Microvision marketing system, as translated for congregational use by the Percept company, provides demographic and psychographic planning information for use in congregations. In this marketing system each individual located in a separate living unit in every community surrounding a congregation is assigned to one of 50 marketing lifestyle categories that can be differentiated according to preferences and socioeconomic status. These market lifestyle assignments are based on preferences for obtaining information (through TV, radio, or newspapers); purchasing habits; preferred living accommodations; choice of automobiles; preferred forms of religious practice (or lack of religious affiliation); and a host of other observable differences.[7] The kind of demographic and market lifestyle information provided by groups such as Percept is highly specific and highly accurate. It draws clear distinctions between the various subgroups of residents in the communities surrounding our congregations.

Many businesses and services that relate to us daily use this kind of information to understand our needs and to learn how to compete more effectively for our attention and dollars. Increasingly congregations are learning marketing techniques. And although we may at times believe that such practices intrude on our lives and that they encourage others to see us as commodities rather than as persons, for the most part we tend to enjoy and appreciate this attention, which seems personalized. For instance, marketing attention to our preferences helps businesses know which mail-order catalogues to put in our mailboxes. And while it is common to hear people gripe over the quantity of junk mail that arrives daily, it is equally common to see people browsing through catalogues while sipping a cup of coffee. They are enjoying the equivalent an old-fashioned "window-shopping trip"—which once took half a Saturday when the shopper walked the downtown streets.

Today's trip is a quiet, almost meditative time spent thumbing through a favorite catalogue. While we may rail against the dehumanizing effects of this advertising attention, we also appreciate something about advertisers that manage to deliver to our door, or to our TV screen, the very things we most like to look at, purchase, and enjoy.

We have become a nation that claims an identity based on democratic unifying principles, but whose institutions increasingly approach the people through finely drawn differences. Perhaps the best example is radio, an industry that is highly responsive to the demographics of its market in strategy and programming. If you grew up on popular music in the years from 1950 to 1965, or if someone in your household did, you undoubtedly were aware of the weekly radio countdown of the "Top 10" or "Top 40." Consider a 1997 news article by Marc Fisher, staff writer for the *Washington Post*, describing what has happened to the countdown of hits that used to unify teenagers from coast to coast:

> Ever feel that life has become disjointed, fragmented into separate strands of experience according to every possible definition of personal difference?
>
> Here's the ultimate proof of the fraying of American culture into countless categories of identity: Casey Kasem whose "American Top 40" shows once united the nation into one great audience climbing the charts together, now records three separate countdowns for stations with different formats.
>
> Kasem, whose distinctive, high nasal voice, and "long distance dedications" dominated weekend radio in the 1970s and '80s, now does different lists of hits for Top 40, "adult contemporary" and "hot adult contemporary" stations.
>
> Somehow, it takes the thrill out of the drumroll for the No. 1 song if you realize that it is merely top o' the charts among, say, women ages 25 to 39. But, that's the nature of today's demographically divided radio dial. In Washington, there are nearly as many countdown shows as there are music stations.[8]

Fisher's article reports *seven* separate weekly countdown formats designed for the Washington, D.C., media market alone—and that is only for the stations that play popular music.

According to Joseph Turrow, the ability to pay attention to such differences has led the advertising and media industries to a cooperative search

for groups of commonality known as "primary media communities." Says
Turrow: "The ultimate aim of this new wave of marketing is to reach different groups with specific messages about how certain products tie into their
lifestyles. Target-minded media firms are helping advertisers do that by
building *primary media communities*."[9]

Also called "image tribes," these segmented and targeted groups of
consumers with a shared identification by age, gender, race, socioeconomic
standing, or any of a host of other variables are helped to see themselves
and others as separate and distinct groups within the larger American public. We are actively encouraged by the media and advertising industries to
see ourselves as a part of the specific image tribe or primary media community to which we most naturally belong.

For instance, have you noticed the signature logos that show up in the
bottom right-hand corner of your TV screen even during a program? The
TV industry, having watched viewers' behavior, became concerned about
the channel surfing of viewers who use remote controls to flip past channel
after channel in a frantic search for something interesting to watch. But we
seemed to surf so fast that we would bypass even the programs we liked.
Haven't you had the experience of flipping through all 36, 61, 90, or 124
channels of your cable-access provider in a fit of boredom, only to start
surfing all over again because you didn't find anything you wanted to watch?
Observing such behavior, TV programmers added a station or network logo
that would remain in a lower corner of the screen. The logo was supposed
to catch your attention on your way by, so that you might at least more
easily recognize the station as one that often carries programs you watch;
then pause and perhaps stay. Science-fiction fans will, as the theory goes,
spot the sci-fi logo and linger to see if they are interested in the current
offering, while classic movie fans will search for the relevant logo and pause
to consider the movie of the moment.

Curiously, and equally important, the development of pure markets, of
"primary media communities" or "image tribes," depends not only on at-
tracting people of shared interests and needs to one another but equally on
repelling people who don't fit the profile. The sci-fi channel wants surfers
to stop their flipping if they are science-fiction fans. But the programmers
hope that if they are not, the signature logo will carry an equally powerful
message that nonfans should move on. This wish to discourage nonfans is
essential to the pure-market concept. A clear example of the dual movements of attraction and repulsion for pure-market development can be seen

in Turrow's comments about the MTV's commitment to "Beavis and Butthead" and "Ren and Stimpy."[10] Turrow notes that "Beavis and Butthead," a cartoon show about two adolescent males (seen as social misfits by the larger public), attracted MTV's target audience, the 18-to-24-year-old population segment. To the programmers of MTV the value of "Beavis and Butthead" was not only that it attracted their segmented and targeted audience, but that the cartoon show also offended and drove away an older, "irrelevant" audience. In fact, "Beavis and Butthead" would help unwanted viewers move on so that those who were a bit older would, programmers hoped, find VH1, the signature station where 24-to-36-year-olds would find programming and advertising designed for them. Each age cohort would be given its own home. And what was left behind was a "pure market."

A pure market is an easy target for marketing. Pure markets of people brought together by their similarities possess shared life experiences, shared images and notions about what is important, and a shared language that can often be abbreviated into images, metaphors, and symbols that carry a meaning that needs no interpretation within the group. I often ask groups that I work with if they can recall ever watching a commercial and having no idea, even at the end, what product was being advertised. People always laugh and say yes. I point out that they were seeing an ad that was not meant for them. It was a commercial designed for a pure-market group of which they were not a part. And although they did not understand that the final "swoosh" they saw on the screen was a closing sales pitch for Nike, the image tribe to which the commercial was directed was well aware that the excitement and the energy of the images that flashed by were attached to a pair of sneakers.

Congregations Don't Fit the Cultural Mold

The problem is that congregations are not "pure market" organizations. In fact, congregations have been caught in the awkward position of being "impure markets" in a time when people have come to expect that attention will be given to their differences. Turrow's core argument:

> [T]he U.S. is experiencing a major shift in balance between society-making media and segment-making media. Segment-making media are those that encourage small slices of society to talk to

themselves, while society-making media are those that have the potential to get all those segments to talk to each other.[11]

The effect of our segment-making strategies, Turrow says, is to create a situation in which individuals are surrounded by reflections of themselves in ways that legitimize a world defined by their own preferences and needs.[12] Marketers do not try to engage differences, large or small, in ways that negotiate those differences to build a broader sense of community. Rather, people are encouraged through self-interest to separate by similarity with others into the electronic equivalent of gated communities.

To a certain extent, congregations have followed that cultural path of attention to communities of similarity. Congregations often reflect the general social homogeneity that surrounds them. Suburban or urban congregations tend to reflect the setting in which they are found. Congregations also tend to reflect socioeconomic or class stratifications. While there are exceptions, some bold and some subtle, congregations continue to reflect racial and ethnic differences. The old truism, attributed to Martin Luther King, Jr., that Sunday morning is still the most segregated hour of the week, accurately reflects many communities. Nonetheless large differences separate the typical congregation and the current cultural predisposition toward pure markets.

Mostly congregations represent impure markets in a pure-market culture. While often reflecting a level of sameness as measured by large-scale differences such as race and ethnicity, congregations are full of the multiple and subtle differences that marketers are quick to avoid. The organizing principle of congregations is not similarity but shared faith and mutual seeking. The idea that unites a congregation is not the similarity of an image tribe or a primary media unit but a community based on shared faith. While the media culture offers multiple cues and clues to help people separate according to their differences, congregations continually seek ways to call people together, bridging those differences to form larger communities in which issues of seeking faith and living meaningful lives can be informed and enriched by the differences of people's experiences. As congregations bring people together on the basis of a shared faith, they breach differences of age, economics, education levels, professional and workplace boundaries, political affiliation or leaning, gender and sexual orientation, musical preferences, hobbies, avocations, family constellations, and physical attributes and skills. All those differences are used by the media culture to segment, target, and shape us into pure markets to be addressed in deference to our differences.

The end result is that churches and synagogues are among the few remaining places in our culture that consistently house and need to know how to use multiple voices and "languages." I often tell congregational leaders that they need to learn how to be multilingual even if the languages that they speak are all English. In this way congregations play a singular role, holding up "nonmarket values," according to Stephen Carter, the William Nelson Cromwell professor of law at Yale University. Congregations, he adds, need to introduce a level of civility to a common marketplace in which differences compete openly with one another in win-lose fashion.[13]

We now come to the dilemma pitting the ways researchers write much of the literature for congregational leaders against the way leaders need to be read it. Learning and using effective and helpful tools of marketing, market research, and advertising, these researchers and writers have done exceptional work identifying differences in expectations and preferences that people bring to the congregation in their search for faith, meaning, and community. For example, leaders of congregations have become much more articulate and sensitive to the need for formality and structure in worship for most people in their 60s and 70s, and to the need for spontaneity and fluidity in worship for most people in their 20s and 30s. Although this information about differences in groups of people can be researched and reported in pure-market fashion, leaders will be using it in impure settings. It is no wonder that worship leaders who make sudden changes in worship to become more spontaneous and responsive to baby boomers and GenXers are met with howls of disapproval from members of the GI generation whose sense of appropriate formality and decorum in worship is disrupted. Our leaders are not incapable of learning the needs and differences of new people coming to our congregations. But our leaders are baffled at how to incorporate what they have learned in congregations whose worship, program, and community life have been dominated by the needs and preferences of groups that got there first. At a recent conference of nationally recognized church musicians and worship leaders, Ian Evison, director of research and planning at the Alban Institute, noted that we know a great deal about contemporary worship. "The bookshelf on how to worship in new ways is very full," he said. "However, the bookshelf on how to introduce those changes into the congregation is empty."[14]

We can learn about "pure" markets, but we are unsure how to use that information in "impure" congregations. We know what baby boomers look for in congregations, but we struggle with how to put that knowledge into practice when members of the GI cohort are looking over our shoulder, telling us we are doing it wrong. And, as we will discover, compromise is, more often than not, an ineffective way to negotiate the differences.

Unique Challenges for Congregations

If, indeed, congregations are countercultural institutions in an increasingly market-driven culture, and if they hold and express nonmarket values, as Stephen Carter suggests, then leaders of congregations face unique challenges not required of other groups, organizations, or institutions. Briefly, let me note just three of those challenges:

1. Consensus building and decision making
2. Evaluation
3. Missional strategies

Consensus Building and Decision Making

A fairly large Lutheran church in a growing New Jersey community questioned the adequacy of its facilities to meet its needs and plans for ministry with new members coming from the surrounding community. Not surprisingly, opinions differed between the longer-tenured members, who were painfully aware of the substantial debt not yet paid off on their current facility, and recent members, who saw only a small remaining debt and a growing need for space. The church council decided to take the issue of a capital-funds campaign for new facilities to a congregational vote. Council members were surprised and dismayed to see opposing forces working to "pack the house" with members sympathetic to their position.

Often congregational leaders work with the tools and assumptions of an earlier time—methods significantly limited in a time highly sensitive to differences. *Robert's Rules of Order* and decisions by majority vote can work well when a foundation of commonality or unity supports the congregation. These basic decision-making tools, when agreed upon, help us to order our lives and experience together. They give us a structured way to discuss the issues and to arrive at a common destination.

But in a diverse culture in which common destinations or goals cannot be assured in congregational life, older models of decision making often divide differing groups into winners and losers. A congregational meeting over facilities can easily degenerate into a contest whose goal is to defeat the opposition rather than to do ministry.

In light of this tendency, congregational leaders need to spend more time and energy than they used to on building consensus and seeking platforms for dialogue. In November 2000 the Alban Institute and the Texas Methodist Foundation of the United Methodist Church jointly sponsored a focus-group discussion among clergy leaders of large United Methodist congregations in Texas (with average worship attendance over 500). The discussion focused in part on the role of the clergy leader. One insight from the discussion was that these leaders commit inordinate (but appropriate) time and attention to identifying and communicating the vision of the congregation as a means of developing consensus among the church's competing subgroups. At the end of the day some participants recognized that one factor that hindered congregations in directing attention to external efforts, whether evangelism or missional outreach, was the amount of energy leaders needed to give to internal differences in the congregation and the building and nurturing of consensus. A unique challenge for congregational leaders in a congregational countercultural position of "impure marketing" is to lead from consensus at a time in which our cultural environment honors and supports differences. Unlike the comparable leaders of businesses, corporations, or institutions whose employment models are based on clear lines of authority, leaders of congregations must lead from positions of consensus in which they are not given sufficient authority to create that consensus. Our leaders have the complex task of building consensus in volunteer systems where participants can "take it or leave it," can participate or not. Indeed, one of the greatest challenges of leaders is that congregations are voluntary systems in which members always have the choice of belonging or not belonging, supporting or not supporting. How shall a leader lead without the needed organizational authority at a time when consensus is harder to build?

Evaluation

A similarly difficult challenge for congregational leaders is to know how to evaluate, and invite others to evaluate, their leadership and goals. In an earlier time of conformity when a high level of similarity prevailed in our congregations and a strong base of agreement and expectation united members, evaluation was a far simpler task. With a higher level of shared expectation in the congregation, performance by leaders and achievement of goals could be fairly easily and accurately measured by the level of satisfaction in the congregation. If complaints were voiced, one could assume that there were problems. If no complaints were heard, one could assume that no problems troubled the congregation's serenity. In the time before pure markets when only a mass-market approach was in vogue, the driving cultural expectations provided well-known standards of practice by which to evaluate.

But in a marketing culture that segments and targets cohorts in ways that develop competing pure markets, members invite increasingly smaller subgroups to come to our congregations—people whose needs and preferences match those of the current congregation. These groups, culturally persuaded to be aware of their differences, expect to have their needs met. They have been taught by a culture of individualism to complain either in an organized fashion or silently by "voting with their feet" (that is, shopping elsewhere) when their needs and preferences are not met.

This situation would suggest that complaints and a certain level of discomfort necessarily exist in healthy congregations that are managing to be "impure" market communities that invite people to come together across their differences. Evaluation, therefore, can no longer depend upon measures of complaint but must be based on more difficult criteria such as alignment with mission or achievement of stated goals.[15] Congregations must have identifiable goals and a clear sense of their own identity and purpose ("call") to evaluate either their leaders or their mission. We have passed the time when it was acceptable to evaluate our leaders by simple measures of satisfaction apart from the goals the congregation has set.

For example, an Episcopal rector and vestry (governing body) were struggling to respond to the congregation's official women's group, which complained regularly and loudly about the lack of cooperation of younger women in the parish. The number of women's circles in the parish was diminishing. Fewer and fewer women were available and interested in the upkeep of the church's formal parlor, service on the altar guild, or volunteer duties staffing and preparing foods for funerals and receptions at the church. The fact that increasing numbers of women in the church were forming and actively participating in parenting groups, support groups, and study groups fanned some flames of resentment among the older women involved in the more traditional structure. How should this difference in what was expected of women's activities in the congregation be evaluated? How should the rector's and vestry's response be evaluated? Lack of support when the official women's group complains can be interpreted as a failure of leaders to meet the established needs of the parish by neglecting to provide active volunteers for tasks that need to be done. Support for younger women to go their own way can be viewed as success in forming new groups to address the needs and preferences of newcomers to the congregation. We cannot, however, assume that this congregation will function well without complaints and dissatisfaction by women on both sides of the issue. This congregation is clearly an impure market of competing sensitivities and needs in which evaluation must be closely tied to the goals and mission of the congregation.

Since this book focuses on leadership in multigenerational congregations, we should note another dilemma—the tendency to evaluate leaders and programs designed for one generational cohort by the standards and preferences of another cohort. A suburban Presbyterian congregation in Georgia hired a new staff member to work with youth. With the help of good planning and a sensitivity to the youths' schedules and demands, the youth worker spent hours attending sporting events at the nearby high schools, meeting at the local Borders bookstore on weekend afternoons and evenings, and forming small Bible-study groups to meet after school in homes, and in one case, on school property. She was effective at building relationships with youth; the number of young people attached to the ministry she led was growing. After the first year, however, the personnel committee offered a less-than-positive review of her work, citing the absence of a weekly Sunday-evening youth group meeting and the lack of plans for any large group event such as a camping trip.

The older generation of personnel committee members recalled their own youthful experiences and critiqued the staff member for not replicating for their children the events that were memorable from their own youth. Staff and volunteer leaders are commonly caught in this bind with no graceful way to talk about the generational differences in needs or expectations without sounding defensive. This is a classic example of a "double bind."

Gregory Bateson, British-born psychologist and philosopher, in his 1972 classic study called *Steps to an Ecology of Mind*, notes three elements that must be present to hold a person in a true double bind.[16]

- The issue must be important. If the issue is unimportant, people do not feel a double bind because they feel free to disregard the tension or remove themselves from the situation. Evaluation of one's performance as a staff worker or a lead volunteer by a personnel committee or a group of peers is important at any number of levels—one's sense of security, financial stability, feeling of accomplishment and self-worth, or freedom to have open relationships with others in the system.
- At least two messages must be offered that are contradictory and that cannot be held together. In this case, the two messages to the staff person were: (1) We want you to form relationships and increase the contact our congregation has with youth, and (2) we want you to have weekly Sunday evening group meetings and spend your time organizing large group functions and trips. These are contradictory messages because the overloaded schedules of youth do not include unstructured time on Sunday evenings for group meetings. Moreover, the local church is not a natural gathering place for most youth today. For the youth leader to commit time and energy to weekly meetings and large trips would remove her from making contacts and forming relationships with the young people where they are found on their natural schedules—at school events, homes, and community gathering places such as bookstores.
- The person caught between conflicting messages is not allowed to comment on the discrepancies. It is this third element that ensures the real pinch. Unable to discuss the mixed generational ideas and expectations without appearing defensive and self-serving, the youth staff leader in this case sought help from the senior pastor to talk to the personnel committee. The pastor was criticized for not being directive enough with his staff.

The competing and contradictory expectations of generations commonly conspire to create double binds that trap and demoralize staff and volunteers. Evaluation cannot be done by applying the preferences or needs of one generation to the experience of another generation. Evaluation must be guided by clear goals that are appropriate to the generation for which the program, service, or effort is planned. Leaders must be aware of the double binds encountered in situations of multiple preferences. Performance evaluations must be based on agreed-upon goals and not be allowed to succumb to complaints about or arguments for preferences.

Missional Strategies

Finally, I would note a challenge to congregations that is unique to our time, but also experienced by other organizations and institutions. Today attention to segmented differences among people is most easily addressed by small, niche-sensitive organizations or by large organizations that can manage multiple strategies and services appropriate to multiple audiences. Our environment is least friendly to and least manageable by midsize organizations seeking with limited resources to be all things to all people.

The North American experience of congregations, especially Protestant and Jewish, has historically been an experience of small community gatherings. Of the approximately 350,000 Protestant, Catholic, and Jewish congregations in the United States, the overwhelming majority are small. The average attendance at weekly worship across all congregations is 75 people (1998 figures). In many of our historic mainline denominations, a great proportion of congregations were established in a time when distance was a factor and small congregations directly served town or rural centers, or a neighborhood.

Researchers and congregational leaders have become aware that although an abundance of small congregations remains, individuals increasingly join large congregations. In fact, using data gathered by the National Congregations Study, Mark Chaves, associate professor of sociology at the University of Arizona, indicates that while the average congregation has an average attendance of 75 people at worship, the average person attends a worship service with 400 other people.[17] This statistic indicates that although most congregations are small, most people find themselves in large congregations today. More and more North American people continue to join and participate in large congregations. For a rather long list of cultural reasons, large congregations are more attractive to people seeking a congregational home.

This trend toward joining large congregations in a landscape dominated by small and midsize congregations requires, once again, that leaders be more critical in reading and using demographic and generational literature about the needs and preferences of segmented pure markets of people coming to their congregations. Although the information about the community is descriptive and accurate for all congregations in the community, the strategic response of leaders should be size-appropriate to their own congregations.

According to the National Congregations Study report, accessible on the World Wide Web, about 60 percent of congregations today are small (less than 100 average worship attendance), about 33 percent of the congregations are midsize (100 to 350 average worship attendance), and less than 10 percent are large (over 350 average worship attendance).[18] Congregational leaders must understand that congregations of different sizes will quite naturally fare better or worse in the present environment and that their response to the environment must be size-specific.

Large congregations. About 7 percent of today's congregations average more than 350 people in weekly attendance at worship. These congregations are most comfortable and compatible with a culture of pure markets because they are large enough, with sufficient, although stretched, resources to do *additive programming.* As new subgroups are discovered, as additional pure markets are encountered, these congregations most often respond by adding groups, programs, targeted worship services, or staff. The additions allow these congregations to focus their efforts more clearly on subgroups without needing to engage fully the differences of other groups in the congregation. While the whole congregation may be a more inclusive impure market, it is commonly made up of collections of pure markets whose differences are buffered by not being in continuous contact with one another. In other words, these large congregations can more easily manage the differences between pure-market subgroups because they are sufficiently large to keep the demographically or generationally different subgroups at a distance from one another. As new subgroups are attracted, the large congregation is best positioned to respond by *adding* targeted programs or services, often adding new staff or resources to make this happen.

This observation is not meant to suggest that leading large congregations is easy. It is, in fact, challenging for leaders to learn to translate their faith message across widening cultural streams while building shared identity, consensus, communication pathways, and trust—elements that will support community in these large congregations. Nonetheless, the large congregation is most culturally appropriate to today's culture because of its ability to respond to multiple preferences or needs among its members. This cultural fit will continue to support the natural growth of the large congregation in the current environment. These congregations will be able most easily to read and use the literature and resources about generational

pure-market segments and to translate the information directly into programs and services. To that extent, it is for these congregations that the
literature of differentiation is written.

Small congregations. About 60 percent of today's congregations average
fewer than 100 people in worship. These congregations are best positioned
for "niche" strategies that are clearly based on their singular spiritual or
organizational gift or strength. They will tend to draw people seeking that
gift or strength. Consider the character of Curly, the toughened trail boss in
the movie *City Slickers*, a remote, intimidating, wizened leader in this comedy about midlife city dwellers in search of life's missing ingredient. Holding up his index finger, Curly instructs his dude-ranch disciples that happiness in life is to know the one thing that is most important. Having repeated
this advice a number of times, the trail boss is finally asked to tell his visitors
what the "one thing" is. Ah, responds Curly, that's what each person has to
find out—because the "one thing" is different for each individual; and truth
and happiness come to the person who is finally able to know the one most
important thing.

    Small congregations are "one-thing communities" of ministry. Each
has a clear spiritual, organizational, or communal gift that it can find and use
to great advantage. But in a culture of segmented image tribes, congregations cannot be all things to all people and still hope to maintain authenticity.
They can live faithfully in a diverse culture if they are willing to understand
themselves and authentically be themselves, to welcome openly and inte-
grate (the hard challenge for these small congregations) newcomers who
seek what they have.

    Small congregations are like the small neighborhood "niche banks"
springing up to offer personal service in an industry increasingly dominated
by a few megabanks created through a series of mergers. The megabanks
are capturing a market share measured in billions of dollars in assets to
achieve a size that will support an ever-growing array of financial services
and products for investors, corporations, and institutions. Neighborhood banks
cannot hope to compete in providing all of the services and products needed
by this ever-widening pool of customers. But small neighborhood banks are
finding a welcome niche among people who don't need to buy bank stock or
to finance a corporate business plan, but who do need someone who can be
helpful when the checkbook doesn't balance. These neighborhood banks
have employees who remember customers' names and maintain business

hours that fit the lifestyles of their customers. They are not projected to join the merger frenzy or ever to become large banks. They do, however, have an important and increasingly viable place in the banking industry. Similar examples include:

- Small neighborhood food markets that cater to the ethnic tastes of their immediate neighborhood, despite a supermarket industry dominated by larger and larger superstores;
- Small charter schools and specialized private schools in an educational environment dominated by huge consolidated city and county school systems; and
- Local health clinics and small surgery centers that specialize in doing one thing well, serving people who would otherwise be lost in a health-care system dominated by enormous regional hospitals and medical centers that squeeze midsize hospitals out of business.

The current cultural environment seems friendliest to the largest and the smallest of our various institutions, industries, and service providers. The largest are welcome because they can do everything. The smallest are sought out because they can do one thing—and do it well. Small congregations need leaders who can help them discern their "one thing" and learn to do it well as an act of spiritual faithfulness. When reading the rich congregational literature about demographic and generational differences, leaders of small congregations should learn to find the one place where their gift or strength can be used to speak to people with a particular need.

Midsize congregations. About 33 percent of today's congregations average between 100 and 350 people attending weekly worship. Midsize congregations are caught in a pinch. Larger than the small congregations, they are expected, and expect themselves, to speak to multiple subgroups of people. However, they do so with limited resources of dollars, staff, volunteers, and facilities. They are in an awkward position, wanting to follow additive strategies used by the large congregation but lacking adequate resources to do all that is required. These congregations often try to stretch and grow to emulate large congregations with multiple programs for different groups. But without the resources of the large congregation, they end up taking the effort out of the blood, sweat, and prayers of staff, lay leaders, and program volunteers who often work beyond their limits. Like midsize banks, grocery stores, schools, and hospitals, midsize congregations often find the current environment hostile and demanding because of their size.

Midsize congregations and their leaders must be the most cautious in reading the current demographic and generational literature that is based on pure-market assumptions. The available information is richly and descriptively accurate, but the midsize congregation is often not in a position to offer a pure-market response like that of the large congregation. Resources and opportunities are lacking to design a differentiated response to each pure-market subgroup that might walk into the midsize congregation. It is therefore the midsize congregation that must be most strategic in making its choices. The strategic response often requires midsize congregations to follow the cultural lead and target ministry to one or two specific subgroups within their community.

Targeting means "choosing the segments [that] will become the organizational focus for one or more of its programs or ministries. That specific segment becomes the target the organization will aim to reach with its message and activities, and from which it will seek a mutual exchange of value."[19] Targeting also means choosing *not* to offer specific programs or services to segments that might be available to the congregation; to do so would create an overload and a mismatch with the congregation. The midsize congregation is often large enough to see and understand everyone, but not large enough to be everything to everyone. In particular, midsize congregations need to be unusually clear in understanding their vision, goals, and strengths so that they know whom to target for ministry and whom not to target. Midsize congregations need to take care in planning their evaluation strategies. Evaluation must be tied clearly to widely understood and accepted goals. Voices of complaint and disappointment will always be raised in midsize congregations that are not comfortably sized to live in a pure-market culture.

Rediscovering Community

Congregational life is often an "impure" experience of mixed generations and lifestyles in a culture that is finding more sophisticated ways to invite us all into pure-market camps. Each of these camps is told to follow Burger King's clever motto, and to expect to "have it your way." Because congregations call people together to seek a shared faith, they do not easily fit the cultural mold in which everyone can expect to "have it your way."

As we continue our examination of congregations, we will explore in depth the differences between generations in our congregations. These differences have repercussions in the worship, programming, fellowship, and governance of our congregations. Because of the current pure-market culture, however, these generational differences are too often seen by the members of congregations as a contest—a reason to participate in a win/lose atmosphere. Leaders need to understand that their congregations cannot conform to the normative social pressures of pure-market preferences. We need to rediscover the meaning of community in this new culture that no longer supports shared assumptions and behavior as the currency of that community. So let us turn our attention to the congregation and begin to explore how these generational differences are lived out in our own experiences.

CHAPTER 2

Quiet Changes:
The Bimodal Congregation

I have been working professionally in congregations for 30 years. For the first 15, I served as a parish pastor and listened to conversations in which it was clear that the ideas of new church members differed from the ideas of long-term members. Changing a board's regular meeting schedule was cheered by one group and denounced by the other. A proposal to rent out part of the building to house a day-care program for children with disabilities was supported by one faction and, out of fear of damage to the building, fought by the other. What surprised me was that I could not always anticipate which issue, decision, or proposal would result in disagreement between longtime and relatively new members. More than once (a clerical understatement) I complained to my colleagues and listened to their matching complaints about the same dynamic in their congregations. Not surprisingly, we had a name for this conflict: the old guard vs. the new guard. The dynamic and name seemed to have fairly wide currency wherever I went. As people have paid more attention to this tension over the years, a language has developed in which the factions are identified in such descriptive terms as "church loyalists" versus "religious consumers."[1]

For the past 15 years I have been working as a full-time consultant to congregations. I have found that this dynamic is not only common, but often at the center of the conflicts that congregations wanted my help in addressing. The territory was familiar, and I was used to listening to stories in which the new guard unreasonably tried to change things or the old guard unreasonably tried to prevent change. In fact, the topic I address in this chapter will not surprise anyone who has lived and worked in congregations in recent years.

What has surprised me, however, is the quiet change taking place in many congregations to deepen and shape this conversation between long-tenured and short-tenured members. The change has been reflected in the membership profiles of many, if not most, established North American Protestant, Catholic, and Jewish congregations over the past several decades. The conversations and experiences of members reflect this change, but many leaders are unaware of the cultural and congregational roots that make this one of the dominant drivers of congregational life.

Finding the New Shape of Congregations

As a denominational consultant, and then as a senior consultant at the Alban Institute, I have often been invited into congregations to help people sort through conflicts that could not be resolved without external assistance. People have needed help to hold conversations whose topics were too uncomfortable to tackle without the "safety net" of a third party who was seen as neutral and objective. To help a congregation in that position, I had to learn a lot about that congregation quickly. Following a pattern deeply embedded in the practice at Alban, I interviewed large numbers of leaders and members and collected basic data about those interviewees. Staff and key leaders were often interviewed individually. Members were most often interviewed in self-selected groups of 8 to 12 people.

It is not uncommon in this situation for a consultant to interview a large proportion of an active congregation, as well as to listen to a number of inactive or former members. Because the process allowed members to sign up in self-selected groups, I often talked to people who already agreed with one another. After all, if tensions are running high and it's a bit unsafe to speak freely, people will select the safest place to speak—in a group likely to agree with their opinions. As long as the consultant remembers that "it's not over till it's over," and listens carefully and openly to all groups and individuals visited, the issues are usually well surfaced. An added benefit is that the consultant gains a clear view of which persons, groups, and subgroups in the congregation carry certain issues or advance certain positions. Not surprisingly, I heard the old guard/new guard theme expressed frequently in relation to a host of issues and discomforts.

As a part of the regular data gathering I, like my colleagues, would use a brief survey form that asked participants to supply basic information about themselves and to respond to several open-ended questions about the situation in their congregation. One question I asked was how long the participant had been a member of this congregation.

Again, there was not much surprise here. Newer members tended to sit and talk agreeably with other new members, while longer-tenured members tended to sit with other longer-tenured members. Their responses to the open-ended survey forms confirmed the tenure of those in each group.

The surprise came when we calculated frequency distributions on the participant data, and developed membership-tenure graphs. In congregation after congregation a basic pattern was repeated with slight variation. The underlying pattern showed that many established congregations have a rather large cluster of long-term members and a rather large cluster of short-term members. The congregations lack a group of mid-tenured members of similar size. This pattern is known statistically as a "bimodal distribution" and, when graphed, would look like this.

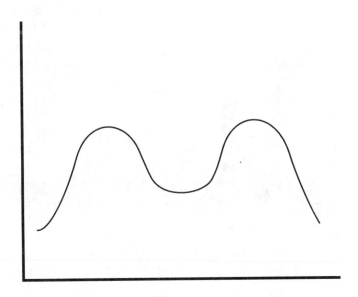

The Bimodal Congregation

"Bimodal congregation" describes the makeup of many congregations and the experience of thousands of congregational leaders with whom I have spoken. Having described the bimodal congregation in seminars, keynote addresses, and consultations for some time, I now find that people intuitively validate the description, saying, "Yes, that's us." As a follow-up, those leaders often do a bit of number-checking to confirm how they fit or vary from the pattern. Many congregations, although sadly not all, have membership records dating back decades, allowing them to determine easily the year in which each member joined. A profile of the membership of a clearly bimodal congregation would look like the following bar graph. On this graph of a congregation with which I consulted, confirmed members are counted in five-year blocks; the blocks are graphed as a percentage of total membership.

Bimodal Congregation

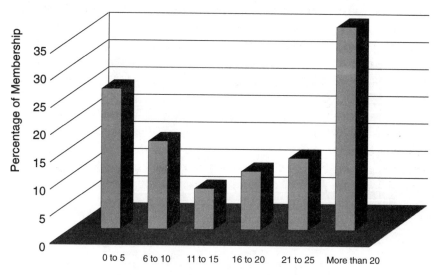

Tenure: Length of Membership in Years

The distribution of members by tenure clearly shows a large group of long-tenured members and a group almost as large of short-tenured members. (In some congregations the short-term group is larger than the long-tenured group.) Whatever the size of these two dominant subgroups, congregations commonly have a "missing group" in the middle.

The missing middle group in congregations is not clearly understood in our investigation of the bimodal congregation. This dip in the middle often represents an age cohort whose numbers in the congregation are much smaller, so that many congregational leaders speak of a "missing generation." For the most part, this smaller group seems to be made up of those in their 40s through mid-50s (in 2001). No data have been gathered specifically on this smallest portion of the membership, but congregational leaders intuitively respond to the hypothesis that this "gap" is the result of baby boomers' rejection of congregations. In his book *A Generation of Seekers*, sociologist of religion Wade Clark Roof notes that the pattern in which adolescents and young adults drift away from congregations and from the religious practice of their parents is well established in American culture. The question is not whether young people move away from religious practice but *whether they return in later life*. Evidence suggests that the baby boomers did not return in the same proportions as earlier and subsequent generations. Influenced by the turmoil of the Vietnam war, cultural trends encouraging self-reliance, and liberation movements that reduced pressures for social conformity, the boomer generation distanced itself from institutions.[2] The boomers' experience may be a significant factor in the dearth of congregation members in the mid-tenure range.

By comparing patterns across congregations for which I had data, I found that a graph in which the subgroups were measured at 10-year intervals most clearly demonstrated bimodal distribution. In this instance, if we describe as long-tenured all members attending a congregation for more than 20 years, we arrive at three subgroups in the distribution.

Bimodal Congregation

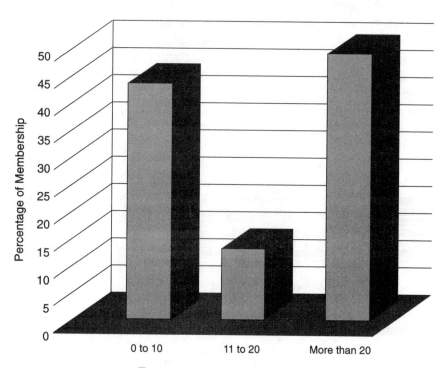

Tenure: Length of Membership in Years

The graph clearly depicts a congregation that has two centers of influence—a long-tenured group and a short-tenured group. When these subgroups are labeled as the old guard and the new guard, we usually separate the terms with "versus." Bimodal congregations speak with two voices. One image: Think of riding in a car with two steering wheels—for sometimes the two centers of influence will seek different paths, and each will grab a steering wheel and hope to move in its preferred direction.

The Heart of the Difference

Leaders need to recognize the critical difference: The two dominant sub-groups operate from *different value systems*. This difference is more than mere disagreement, opposing preferences, an age gap, or the tension of new ideas meeting established practices. The difference between short-tenured and long-tenured members that leads to friction is the contrast be-tween the two groups' cultural value systems. These two groups may look similar; they may come from the same families and neighborhoods. But they hold sharply differing assumptions about life that confound them when they gather as a congregation.

It is important to understand that members of each group really *like* the people in the other group, and they consciously choose to be with one another. Leaders must not miss or undervalue the attraction that the two groups have for one another. Obviously, there is a high correlation between one's length of membership in a congregation and one's age. Longer-ten-ured members tend to be older; short-tenured members tend to be younger. These age differences often support the two groups' interest in being with one another.

For the older subgroup, the younger group represents energy and new ideas; fresh volunteers to carry on meaningful work; added financial and time resources to keep the congregation going. To the older eye, the younger people represent a future through which an institution of great meaning in the older members' lives will be continued. It is not inconsequential that the newer, younger members bring their children. Ours is an increasingly mo-bile society in which fewer and fewer adults live in the community in which they grew up. That means that many grandparents live long distances from their grandchildren. An older person whose offspring have moved halfway across the continent can seldom sit in a worship service with a granddaugh-ter or tease with a grandson across the fellowship table at a congregational dinner. It is with relief and pleasure that the older subgroup in our congrega-tions can sit with and play with the children of the congregation's younger members. Indeed, the older and longer-tenured members appreciate being able to share their congregation with the newer and younger participants.

Similarly, the younger and shorter-tenured members have an affection and appreciation for the older, longer-tenured subgroup. The older folk rep-resent stability of resources and institutional commitment. They represent an affirmation of a valuable heritage passed from generation to generation.

They also represent resident wisdom about life. In this mobile society young adults can seldom sit at the kitchen table with their own parents and grandparents to listen to wise stories of managing family life or career. The congregation is one of the few remaining formal or informal institutions in our culture that invite people of different generations to sit together and to share stories and discoveries about life. Many younger members are drawn to that setting because of the opportunity to come to a communal kitchen table of wisdom and, if not to engage their elders in conversation, at least to observe them in this congregational habitat.

As leaders of congregations, we need to remind ourselves continually that these groups do actually like each other and that they choose to be with one another although one set is "old guard" and the other "new guard." Leaders need to understand also that, despite this amicability, these groups *do not speak well with each other.* They confuse one another.

The problem is that the old guard and the new guard, representing two or more cultural or generational value systems, use similar words and language to mean quite different things. These people have been trained to see, to think, and to talk about things differently—even though they may use the same words.

Generations' Value Differences

Being part of a generation is more than simply sharing an age or approximate age with other people. It also encompasses shared life learnings and a cultural predisposition to understand your experience in ways similar to your age-mates, or those born a few years earlier or later. The word "cohort" has the root meaning of an "enclosed company" of people. Sociologists commonly refer to generational differences by describing generational cohorts—enclosed companies of people who have in common certain formative experiences and lessons that shape their response to life.

William Strauss and Neil Howe are writers and lecturers on generational issues, particularly as they relate to the cyclical patterning of our culture's changing value structures. They found that the length of a generation in American history averages about 21 years (before the early 19th century a generation averaged about 25 years). Strauss and Howe note that the length of a generation can vary, depending on the historical context and the timing of significant events. Certain shared experiences, sets of assumptions, and life learnings shape each generation differently. Each generation has its own story, its own personality. In *The Fourth Turning*, Strauss and Howe write:

> To apply these lengths to real birth years, you have to locate an underlying generational persona. Every generation has one. It's a distinctly human—and variable—creation, with attitudes about family life, gender roles, institutions, politics, religion, lifestyle, and the future. A generation can think, feel, or do anything a person might think, feel or do. It can be safe or reckless, individualist or collegial, spiritual or secular. Like any social category (race, class, or nationality), a generation can allow plenty of individual exceptions and be fuzzy at the edges. But unlike most other categories, it possesses its own personal biography.[3]

No matter how similar the circumstances and environment for the generational subgroups in our congregations and communities, their preferences, assumptions, attitudes and decisions are shaped by the distinct generational biographies that are shared intensely within the generation but not fully shared across generations.

Strauss and Howe suggest three attributes that contribute to a distinct generational persona: a common location in history, common beliefs and behavior, and a perceived membership in the common generation. Picking up on the theme of common location in history, Wade Clark Roof, the J. F. Rowny professor of religion and society at the University of California in Santa Barbara, notes the work of an early sociologist, Karl Mannheim, who wrote of common location in the social process.

> More than just an aggregate of individuals of a similar age, a generation thus tends to have a common, unifying social experience and to develop a collective sense of identity. Members of one age group define themselves in relation to other cohorts by rejecting or reaffirming one or another set of cultural values, beliefs, and symbols; in this way a generation comes to have its own distinctive "historical-social" consciousness. This is likely to occur in late adolescence and early adulthood—the formative years for the shaping of a distinct outlook.[4]

For a generational cohort's development, it makes a substantive difference when one was born and what messages one received while growing up. If one was born in the 1910s or '20s and came to adulthood during World War II, the leadership of General (and later President) Dwight D. Eisenhower might exemplify the generational messages of conformity and belonging. For example, Eisenhower declared, "Our government makes no sense unless it is founded in a deeply felt religious faith—and I don't care what it is."[5] What a person believed was not as important to Ike as membership in a group that believed *something*.

Belonging and conformity were more dominant values even than religious belief or practice of spiritual disciplines. Not coincidentally, the values of belonging and conformity were key values at that historical moment, underscoring the importance of group life. A sense of belonging and conformity got one through a world war, helping to establish a stable nation and economy to follow. The values of belonging and conformity and the need for cultural stability would be fundamental lessons that shaped a generation's response to daily activities and to personal and community decisions. These values would have an obvious impact on participation and decision making in community institutions such as a congregation.

However, if one was born in the 1940s or 1950s and reached young adulthood in the 1960s or '70s, the messages and experiences would be quite different. To witness on TV the assassination of a popular, almost heroic young president, to watch the dinner-hour news reports of televised battle losses in an unpopular war, and to come of age hearing the cultural chant "If it feels good, do it"—these events would produce an effect very different from that experienced by the earlier generation. Stability would be neither felt nor required. Conformity and belonging would give way to cultural values of individuality, self-interest, and self-protection. The life lessons and generational cultural values would be different for this group. And the impact on participation and decision making in community institutions such as congregations would also diverge from the past.

Life lessons and shared experiences determine the most basic responses of generational cohorts. Having experienced shared events and learning, each generational cohort has its own language and place in history that cannot easily be understood or shared by other cohorts. Rabbi Lawrence Hoffman, co-director of Synagogue 2000, a cross-denominational program of synagogue transformation, emphasizes the idea that a common location is a generational marker by defining a "project" as another way people of common experience determine their place in history.[6]

A project is something greater in scope and design than our own individual work or effort. In a project we join a cause that stands for something larger than ourselves, such as a war or a civil rights movement—one that will leave a legacy and a history for others to follow. This participation in a cause larger than ourselves gives us a context to understand ourselves and to contribute to a greater whole. Generational cohorts, with their unique histories and shared experiences, invest themselves in distinctive projects.

The bottom line is that otherwise similar people of different ages can have sharply contrasting life experiences, even as they live side by side in the same family, community, or congregation. Representing several generations, the people in our congregations are brought together by a choice to be with one another; but then they are confounded by their inability to understand one another or to find ready agreement on even the most basic questions.

This confusion between groups is not a question of mean, miserable people in our congregations failing to get along because they are unreasonable or nasty. At times, of course, we see evidence of difficult and inappropriate behavior as members disagree and revert to win-lose tactics because they lack the needed alternative skills. For the most part, our congregations are made up of people who enjoy and appreciate each other. Nonetheless, they are baffled by subtle and shaded differences that allow them all to use the same words but to impute different meanings to them, that allow them to have common goals but to disagree on strategies to accomplish them. These members are doing the best they can, working with their own generational cohort's life learnings. Not surprisingly, they can more easily enlist agreement and cooperation from people of their own generational cohort; they are confused by the lack of understanding and response from other cohorts that routinely seem to miss the point.

In the bimodal congregation, each center of influence—the long-tenured cluster and the short-tenured cluster—carries the value system of a different generational cohort. They share a search for a sense of community and a relationship with God. But the shape of the search, the means for getting there, and the ideas and decisions that drive each group differ subtly and stem from different life lessons.

Observations of the Bimodal Congregation

The bimodal congregation will be explored in greater detail in subsequent chapters. For the moment I share four basic observations about this shape in congregational membership and life. I hope these four observations will help leaders more easily come to two early conclusions:

1. Much of the present discomfort and tension in our congregations is normal and healthy. Far from being a problem to be solved, it is normative. Leaders need to release themselves from the bind of believing that they should be able to make everyone happy. Rather, leaders need to find ways to appreciate and use the natural tension in these congregations to engage the opposing voices in conversation about purpose and identity—issues of congregational vocation and call.
2. A bimodal congregational profile is good news. It is a sign of health and promise for the future.

And now, the observations:

1. *Values are not easily negotiated.* One of my father-in-law's favorite lines in "spousal discussion" with his wife was, "Jane, I never argue unless I know I'm right." As far as an argument goes, that's a showstopper. If I know that I'm right, then the argument is over, since to give in would be to confuse error and truth. The line was favored in conversations in my family because it was always said with a bit of a smile and a twinkle in the eye.

However, when negotiating agreement, simply knowing that one is right is "positional arguing," say Roger Fisher and William Ury in their famous report of the Harvard Negotiation Project. Positions are the conclusions that people reach and hold that are often non-negotiable. Positionally oriented people conclude that a particular action or decision is simply right, and any other position is unacceptable. According to Fisher and Ury:

> When negotiators bargain over positions, they tend to lock themselves into those positions. The more you clarify your position and defend it against attack, the more committed you become to it. The more you try to convince the other side of the impossibility of changing your opening position, the more difficult it becomes to do so.

Your ego becomes identified with your position. You now have a new interest in "saving face"—in reconciling future action with past positions—making it less and less likely that any agreement will wisely reconcile the parties' original interests.[7]

The competing value systems in our congregations often provide the basis for positional arguments and disagreements. A subgroup that holds a particular value simply sees its way as right and does not understand why it should consider a different way.

The primary insight here for leaders is that continually explaining one group's positions to the other is not often productive. The assumption is false that continual explanation will persuade people to change their minds. Repeated efforts simply push people deeper into their uncompromising positions. We should not miss the fact that persuasion is a dominant strategy by which leaders (especially males) in our culture deal with differences. In Speed Leas's self-report instrument *Discover Your Conflict Management Style*, which offers measures of preferred ways to deal with conflict, persuasion is the dominant style of male laity and the second-ranking style for clergy (after collaboration).[8] But attempts to persuade others that one of two competing value systems is "right" tend to fail. As we will see in exploring the bimodal congregation more deeply in the following chapters, compromise is often impossible and, when attempted, unsatisfying.

The differences in basic assumptions run deep in the multiple value systems held in our congregations. Direct attempts by leaders to find compromises, solve problems, and find winners often add to the problem. Simply understanding the multiple value systems is a more productive activity, and helping people talk to one another across their differences is a major responsibility of leaders. It should not surprise us that leaders must spend so much time and effort building consensus in our congregations.

2. *The dominant value systems in most established congregations are defined by the GI and baby boom generations.* As noted in chapter 1, a great reification of generational differences is being defined through pure-market methodologies. Clearer differences between generational cohorts are being described so that early baby boomers and late baby boomers are now seen as distinct from each other, as are GenXers and millennials, with a number of shadings to be found between these larger generational categories. It is possible, especially for large congregations, to attend to all

of these shadings and to design ministry that speaks more naturally and effectively to specific generational cohorts. One effective strategy for a new congregation is to clarify which generational cohorts it is called to address in its developing ministry.

In my experience, however, for the overwhelming majority of established congregations, the primary cultural value differences to be negotiated are those separating the GI generation and the baby boomers. The boomers began the shift to what I will call the consumer-value system. The GI generation's value system has been a dominant presence in established congregations because of the heroic identity that it established during World War II. The GI dominance is also supported by the congruence between mainline Protestant theology and the GI generation's insistence on personal responsibility—a value in line with the Protestant work ethic. The dominance of this value system is further supported by the sheer number of people in this cohort who have been and continue to be primary leaders in the congregation.

In response to the dominant presence of a GI cultural value system, the baby boomers introduced a new value system that has been adopted with variations by succeeding generational cohorts, even as the younger cohorts have sought to correct and balance the boomers' world view. The result is that many established congregations—Protestant, Catholic, and Jewish— still find themselves negotiating the primary cultural value differences between the GIs and the subsequent consumer-driven cohorts. This observation is supported by the generational research of Jackson Carroll, project director of Pulpit & Pew: Research on Pastoral Leadership at Duke Divinity School.

> The major generational watershed, as far as religious beliefs and practices are concerned, is between those who in our research we call Pre-boomers (born prior to 1946) and those who have come after. Although Boomers (born 1946-1964) and Xers (born 1965-1979) differ in some respects, they are much more like each other than like Pre-boomers.[9]

The GenX and the millennial cohorts are, in fact, exceedingly different from the baby boomers. But the GenXers and millennials will have even more trouble finding a comfortable home in many established congregations than their baby-boomer parents have had. To that extent, the future viability and vitality of our congregations are challenged as spiritual communities able to nurture people of faith in these generational cohorts. But it is clear from my experience in working with established congregations that unless we learn how to negotiate the differences between the GI cohort and the boomers, we have little hope of negotiating the generational differences and changes represented by succeeding cohorts.

3. *Our congregations are currently shaped for discomfort.* Not to be missed is the fact that even our healthiest congregations are structured to be uncomfortable. As later chapters will make clear, a host of ideas, programs, and decisions face our congregations. The various subgroups cannot be expected to find agreement on these. Hence, the more fully a congregation is able to include new generational cohorts in its membership and leadership, the more it is institutionally contributing to its own discomfort. To the surprise and dismay of many, this natural state of discomfort—which requires that leaders give increased attention to internal differences—stands in stark contrast to the comfort and agreement that congregations are remembered to have enjoyed only a few decades ago.

The current state of discomfort in many congregations is exacerbated by the missing subgroup in the middle. As we saw in the chart on page 40, a congregation with bimodal distribution of members can count, between the two larger clusters of short-tenured and long-tenured members, a much smaller group, people who have been members from 11 to 20 years. The mid-tenured group may be too small to buffer the differences between the two large subgroups on either side. Few members are close enough to each of the large subgroups to understand and interpret their differences. With an insufficient number of bridge people to translate, the bridging task falls inordinately to staff and to key lay leaders who, by virtue of their leadership positions, live in this in-between space, whatever their own length of membership may be.

4. *The bimodal congregation is evidence of denominational growth and congregational relevance.* Beginning in the 1970s, the mainline denominational bodies of our various faith traditions have become sensitive to a membership decrease, which has continued unabated for several decades. Voices far and wide have eagerly offered explanations for this persistent trend. Reasons theological, political, cultural, social, and ecclesiological have been suggested. No doubt each explanation has some truth to contribute. However, others pointing to that trend have prematurely announced the death of mainline denominations, established congregations, traditional

worship, or congregations other than those that are large and culturally congruent.

However, the dominance of the bimodal congregation as a model offers new insight into the viability and vitality of established congregations that some have too easily dismissed. That many congregations include a large cluster of short-tenured members suggests that when we open the doors, people do come—and not just the same people who have always come.

Assuredly, some in the short-tenured subgroup have transferred from other established congregations because of a job or residence change, or because of dissatisfaction with their previous congregation. Yet the story is more complex than that. An increasing number of people come to established congregations looking for their first congregational home, or come with no prior congregational or faith experience. The growing cluster of the short-tenured also includes constituents not counted as members in the bimodal model, because they do not choose to go through formal procedures for becoming a member. A growing percentage of people participate actively in congregations but do not seek and will not accept membership. Yet their commitment to spiritual seeking and to the congregation appears to be as deep as the commitment of those who hold formal membership.

Mainline denominational membership losses have not subsided. In general, the average age of membership in established congregations tends to be significantly higher than the average age in the population at large. The average age of confirmed members in the United Methodist Church in the U.S., for example, is approximately 57 years, compared to the median age of 35.3 for the U.S. population in general. This statistic suggests that in such denominations net losses from deaths will continue in the immediate future at a level that cannot be exceeded by gains from births and new members to achieve net growth. Nonetheless, signs other than net growth indicate health and vitality and suggest that many established congregations are healthy, open systems that still receive and serve new worshipers. For example, a number of mainline denominations are now pointing not to increased membership but to increased average worship attendance as a pattern over the past few years.[10] Although we do not have the final evidence that would allow us to describe the developing American religious landscape accurately, it is clear that the bimodal profile is evidence of health and a viable future for many established congregations. This finding suggests that the bimodal congregation is well worth investigation and attention.

CHAPTER 3

Biblical Glimpses
of Congregational Life

What can be said about the spiritual life of bimodal congregations? Most of the description and interpretation brought to the bimodal congregation in this book comes from the social sciences, systems theory, and the experience of working with leaders in real-life decision-making situations. Daily life in a congregation has a sense of immediacy that seems best explained by the tools of our sciences and an analytic mode. The sights, sounds, and smells of close human encounter will often suggest a distance from the biblical and spiritual truths that are meant to be conveyed by life in these congregational communities.

In his memoir of his first pastoral call in southern Illinois, Professor Richard Lischer of Duke Seminary recalls the impromptu wedding, the counseling sessions that led to reconciliation, the hateful accusations spoken by a member in anger, the prayers and confessions—all of which took place in his study while he was pastor of a small rural congregation. Connecting that daily stuff of real-life encounters with the faith that it represents, he writes: "That room contained our community's version of faith, conflict, and love."[1] It takes the continual work of leaders to connect the daily moments of congregational life to the large landscape of the biblical record. Each congregation has its own version of that connection.

The bimodal congregation is a spiritual community in temporal space. Called together through shared faith, members need help in daily living to stay connected to the congregation's biblical purpose as part of a larger tradition, and need help to stay connected to the vision or mission that called the congregation into being. Regular monthly board meetings seldom reflect this connection well. Yet negotiating the bimodal differences in a congregation is a deeply spiritual function that keeps both faith and community alive. I have been convinced of the spiritual nature of this negotiation as I work as a consultant to congregations deeply enmeshed in their differences. One of my favorite and most productive exercises with leaders is to invite them to find the biblical story that their congregation is living at that moment. I invite them to find their spiritual space by locating the biblical story in which they see themselves—the story or idea in the text that they would intuitively say "describes us."

This is neither a literal nor a historically critical way of approaching Scripture. The exercise is metaphorical play—but deeply spiritual play that can instruct us in new ways. Old Testament theologian Walter Brueggemann has offered the exile experience of the Israelites as one of the most productive metaphors for the current state of faith in the United States. His reflection on the metaphorical power of Scripture inspires leaders to connect the mundane and often frustrating experience of daily life in community with the biblical promise that makes it purposeful.

The usefulness of a metaphor for rereading our own context is that it is not claimed as a one-on-one match to "reality," as though the metaphor of "exile" actually described our situation. Rather a metaphor proceeds by having only an odd, playful, and ill-fitting match to its reality, the purpose of which is to illuminate and evoke dimensions of reality that will otherwise go unnoticed and therefore unexperienced.[2]

The exercise I use is simple and straightforward. I invite a small group of leaders to find the story they are now living and, when they return to the group, to explain why they believe they are living that story. I will often expand the possibilities, allowing the group to use a denominational hymnal if they prefer to find the hymn they are living. Some congregations and individuals are more sensitive to sound and music than to words or word pictures. I usually give the group an hour for its work. Many groups need more time.

The conversations of these groups are rich and instructive (I listen in when I have the opportunity). People go through their own personal repertoire of Bible stories looking for a connection. Fragments of stories are recalled, and people begin flipping through the pages in search of the full story. When the proposed stories are found in the text, they are read aloud. Details long forgotten or never known are discovered. As the stories are read, it is the details that convince. Listening to the reading, the group will often conclude that something about the story fits, but "it isn't really us." And then, one or more times, the details will connect and the moment of insight will hit the group. I once worked with a group of leaders in a troubled church who returned from their assignment with the announcement that they had found five stories that belonged to them—two that they wished they were living and three that they wished they were not living. I would argue that their hour or so of spiritual leadership in discerning their biblical place was more "centering" and helpful than the many hours of organizational leadership they had committed to solving people's problems. Without the biblical connection they had been working hard to become good leaders in a difficult situation. With the biblical connection they shifted to the behavior of spiritual leaders and found their responsibility to be much more purposeful.

I am often surprised at how accurately the story chosen by a small group lays open the bimodal motif that rests at the heart of their differences. When the story is claimed by the larger leadership team, it becomes the focus of Bible study for the full group. The Bible study may include textual criticism, or it may be playful or introspective. Once the story is found, I encourage the leaders not to leave it until it is fully digested.

Beginning in this brief chapter and interspersed among subsequent chapters are three bimodal biblical stories identified and lived out by congregations. The other chapters continue to use social-science tools and a systems approach to describe the dynamics of congregations. The biblical stories are told to keep in the reader's mind the spiritual life negotiated in these congregations. As Brueggemann suggests, the stories are metaphors to be played with. Ill-fitting but accurate, they are told in the congregation not with the aim that people learn more about the Bible but so that through the biblical story the people may know more about themselves and their purpose.

The first story was claimed by a Protestant congregation amid planning by the governing board. I was invited to work with the board over two weekends several months apart, and we agreed that a self-study of congregational data and introduction to big-picture cultural dynamics (see the discussion of balcony work in chapter 9) would fill a part of our time together. As a part of the self-study, the leaders were asked to prepare a tenure study of their members and other participants; the resulting graph was a clear example of bimodal distribution. As we explored their bimodal graph, I asked the leaders to place themselves on the graph by their own length of membership or participation. We discovered that fully 85 percent of the leaders at the center of this congregation were long-tenured members of 20 years or more. Only 12 percent had been members between 10 and 19 years and fit into the smaller middle segment. Only one person within the core leadership had been active in the congregation for less than 10 years, though a substantial portion of active members and other constituents of the congregation were short tenured. Clearly the leadership group did not reflect the makeup of the membership. Much of our planning was focused on the leaders' concern over the apathetic response they had received over the past few years to the congregation's traditional programs and projects.

Asked to find their biblical story, a small group of leaders set off somewhat reluctantly but came back with high enthusiasm. They had found the postresurrection story of the appearance of Jesus in the 21st chapter of John (John 21:1-12) and claimed it as their own. This account of the disciples after the crucifixion shows them standing at a lakeside not quite knowing what to do or expect. Impetuous Peter announces that he is going fishing; he is joined by the other disciples in an all-night fishing expedition. Having caught nothing all night, the disciples are hailed by a stranger from the shore—later revealed to be Jesus. The stranger instructs them to cast their nets on the other side of the boat. Doing so, they haul in a catch of 153 fish (which, I later learned, represented one of every type of fish known at that time). In encountering Jesus and in shifting their nets from one side of the boat to the other, they went from catching nothing to catching one of every kind of fish.

When I asked these leaders why this story struck them as theirs, they pointed to our planning work and to the fact that 85 percent of the leaders at this church were long tenured, coming from only one side of their bimodal "boat." It had become clear to them that they knew how to fish only out of one side of the boat, following the preferences of the established GI cohort of leaders. This insight helped them see why they had been getting an increasingly smaller response to their traditional programming. "If we hope to catch anything in the future," one said, "we are going to need to learn how to fish out of the other side of the boat."

The leaders still faced a significant challenge of changing well-established behavior and expectations. But where our work might have bogged down in organizational diagnosis, this group exercised spiritual leadership and discovered a much clearer reason to redesign their leadership-development process to meet their new bimodal needs.

CHAPTER 4

Looking at the Parts

Congregations are doing ministry in the context of a "major generational watershed," as noted by Jackson Carroll in chapter 2. This major divide separates "preboomers"—that is, people born before 1946—from those who came after. "Watershed" is an appropriate and helpful image. The term denotes a ridge or high place dividing a large geographic area drained by different rivers or river systems. (The continental divide is one such.) I live near such a watershed in Pennsylvania. On one side the water drains west toward the Susquehanna River and into Chesapeake Bay; on the other side the water flows east toward the Delaware River and into the Delaware Bay. Surely the rain that falls in a particular place flows in multiple directions depending on immediate elevations and ground slope. However, gravity ensures that the overall flow of water from the watershed divides, headed eventually toward one bay or the other.

The "watershed" within bimodal congregations has similar qualities. Preferences about any decision or practice in the congregation may flow in many directions at one time. As with local water, multiple variables will influence the immediate flow. However, dominant and more determinant flows or pulls will direct a large portion of the behaviors and attitudes within the congregation. The dividing lines for congregations tend to be generational value systems, which function much like the watersheds that determine the flow of water from the large masses of a geographical area.

As noted earlier, it is possible, using a pure-market approach, to differentiate specifically the preferences of generational cohorts such as GIs, early boomers, late boomers, Xers, and millennials. However, congregations more often find themselves negotiating the more basic differences between two primary cultural value systems marked by the "watershed" of the birth year 1946.

This dominant value distinction to be negotiated is the difference between the *GI value system* and the *consumer value system*. Using that watershed distinction to identify differences, the bimodal congregation can be interpreted through the three basic subgroups identified in chapter 3.

* The GI generation value cohort (pre-1946)
* The consumer generation value cohort (post-1946)
* The bridge people

Before we describe the bimodal congregation more closely, please recognize that this is an exercise in simplification. I acknowledge to the reader, as I do to congregational leaders with whom I work, that we are embarking on a conversation about people and groups in the congregation, described in a stereotypical manner. I further recognize that for almost any statement describing the values, behaviors, and preferences of subgroups within congregations, one can probably point to specific examples to the contrary. Nonetheless, leaders need to have a clear sense of the basic value differences that mark significant groups within congregations; through these the smaller and more confusing differences can be understood. The differences in the value structures of the GI and the consumer generational cohorts in congregations can be described using four "markers":

* Deferred pleasure vs. instant gratification
* Group vs. individual orientation
* Assumptions of sameness vs. difference
* Spirituality of place vs. spirituality of pilgrimage

Exploring Generational Cohorts and Their Markers

In reading these descriptions, keep in mind that they point to life lessons that differ from one generational cohort to another. The question is not whether one of set of values is better than another, but whether we can understand the values as life lessons appropriate to the people who went through critical developmental life stages when these value systems were dominant.

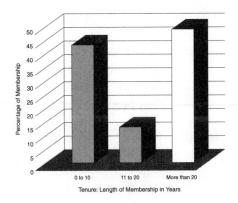

Tenure: Length of Membership in Years

The GI Generation Value System

1. Deferred Pleasure

Let's begin this description of the GI generation value system with the marker of deferred pleasure, since it rests on a fundamental and broadly shared experience in the American setting. It can be understood through the American "giving/getting compact," described by noted market researcher Daniel Yankelovich as the "unwritten rules governing what we give in marriage, work, community and sacrifice for others, and what we expect in return."[1] The giving/getting compact that was central to the experience of people born before the 1946 divide was formed primarily by the Protestant work ethic: One did what was required in the current moment, and one delayed gratification for a future time when the reward would be appropriate.

Under this value system it was common practice for people to commit their labor to one company or industry for their full adult working lives. My grandfather, for example, began working for the Lehigh Valley Railroad at age 13. He remained with that railroad until he retired at age 65, when he reaped the promised rewards of a gold watch and a pension that would see him and my grandmother through the rest of their lives. That meant committing his working years to one company through good and bad, through agreement and disagreement, with a sense of responsibility and sacrifice. My grandfather could make that commitment with a belief that reciprocity or payoff would come in the rewards that would allow him to care for his family, buy and own a home, and live with a sense of control and security.

Such lifelong commitment is much like the "heroism of midlife" that *Boston Globe* columnist Ellen Goodman identified in a column about the popularity of the movie *Groundhog Day*. The film comedy centers on a TV weather forecaster sent to Punxsutawney, Pennsylvania, to report on the February 2 weather forecast, to be determined by whether the ground-hog "Punxsutawney Phil" sees his shadow. The weather guy (Bill Murray) finds himself trapped in seemingly endless repetitions of February 2, each a virtually identical Groundhog Day. Morning after morning, he awakes to a clock radio playing Sonny and Cher's rendition of "I've Got You, Babe." The exasperating replays of February 2 end only when the Murray charac-ter learns to exchange his boorish, selfish behavior for more responsible and appropriate conduct befitting an adult—thus earning the love and respect of the woman he has fallen for (Andie McDowell). Only then can he move on to February 3. Goodman's description of the movie as a metaphor for the heroism needed to address the humdrum dailyness of life is a good example of the pre-1946 giving/getting compact. Whereas the years of youth and young adulthood are marked by choice—of mate, educational path, career, and location—Goodman notes that the heroism of midlife is remaining faith-ful to and responsible for the choices already made. Midlife is a time of commitment to the unvarying days that come as a consequence of choices made when one was younger, a daily commitment whose rewards will not be given right away but realized only over the long haul. The GI generation understood and accepted the concept of deferred pleasure, requiring daily responsibility and sacrifice, whose full rewards would not be reaped until some later time.

This value system of deferred pleasure, known variably as the Protes-tant work ethic or the American way of life, spoke *the language of re-sponsibility*. One's value and place in the community were measured by one's ability to be responsible and dependable toward commitments made and roles accepted. The valued husband or father was one who could "put a roof over his family's head." The valued church member was one who attended worship regularly, pledged regular financial support, and could be expected to show up for committee meetings. Immediate pleasure was not expected but rather deferred to a time when the present sacrifices and responsibilities would produce the intended results.

Because of this willingness to defer personal pleasure and gain and because of the sense of personal responsibility, it should not be a surprise that both the Social Gospel and the Great Society were religious and politi-cal expressions of this value system. In both cases, the underlying belief was that present sacrifices through the giving/getting compact would result in a better world, or a closer approximation of the kingdom of God.

The GI generation's value system also brought a sense of responsibility to the congregation. To be a member of a congregation was also to be a good citizen to the larger community, a good spouse, and a good parent. Membership in this group is defined or measured by the amount of time, money, and attention sacrificed for the good of the whole. Not surprisingly, those who live closest to the cultural lessons of deferred pleasure point easily to responsibilities that are not equally perceived or accepted by newcomers to the congregation. It is common to hear this long-tenured group of members say that they have carried out their responsibilities long enough and "now it is time for others to step up and keep things going." Later, when we look at the value system of the consumer generation, it will be clearer why newer and younger members do not simply step into the roles, positions, and responsibilities of the group born before 1946. But it should not be missed that the assumption that newer people need to pick up the responsibilities of longer-tenured members is frequently based on an expectation that the newcomers should maintain the established patterns of the congregation rather than initiating changes. An attendant assumption within the GI generation value system specifies that once the path or pattern of how to do things has been determined, people should keep doing it the same way. That statement leads us to the second generational marker—a group identity.

2. The Group Identity of the GI Generation

The pre-1946 generational cohorts in our congregation tend to see themselves as a group. As cyclical historians William Strauss and Neil Howe note:

> The initials "G.I." can stand for two things—"general issue" and "government issue"—and this generation's lifecycle has stood squarely for both. All their lives, the G.I.s have placed a high priority on being "general" or "regular" (as in "he's a regular guy"), since regularity is a prerequisite for being effective "team players." They developed this instinct young, building in high school and college what historian Paula Fass labels a "peer society"—a harmonious community of group-enforced virtue.[2]

The life lesson that supported this group identity and cohesion—the sense of team—came from the chaotic and threatening environment of the Great Depression and World War II. The cultural lesson was to band together and to take on these great threats as full communities or as a nation, that is, as a group. It has been said that the learned response to problems for the GI generation was to identify the problem, to find out who was on your team by looking for people like you who agreed with you, to focus on the solution, and never to give up. The life lesson was that if you followed this path, you could do anything, even win a world war.

I have jokingly said to leaders that these are the people in your congregation who show up without an appointment at the denominational executive's office in a rented bus with a petition stating that they are displeased with what is going on in their congregation. In several instances this example turned out not to be a joke, since it was a fairly accurate description of what happened when a congregation was dealing with seemingly unresolvable differences.

I recall in particular working in several congregations where long-tenured members held secret "by-invitation-only" meetings to organize their displeasure. In each case I identified these secret meetings and described them publicly as unhelpful to the decision making and community building that we were working on for the whole congregation. In each case, some long-tenured members expressed surprise that I would object to what they were doing, since they assumed it was the way people naturally handled such situations. Secret meetings among people who already agree are, in fact, unhelpful since they break communication between the people who need to be talking— and listening—to each other. However, leaders should recognize that GI-oriented folk are not mean-spirited people trying to defeat the opposition unfairly. Rather, these people are using their life lessons as a group-oriented cohort that long ago learned the effectiveness of a coordinated team with a strategy to accomplish what they believe to be "right."

Leaders should understand that those who hold the GI value system tend to have a clear idea of what is "right" and believe that "right" is determined by the group. For these members, there is a right way and a wrong way to do many things, and the "right" is determined by what is good for the group. The driving assumption is that if there is a right way to worship, then it is the right way for *everyone* to worship. Multiple worship services designed to speak to different groups, and blended worship that brings together traditional liturgy with personal testimony or praise music, are not natural starting places for this group when its members think about making their worship "better." Another driving assumption: There is a right way to build a budget and support it, and it is based on the principle that everyone pays a fair share toward an agreed-upon program agenda. The driving assumption of mission or outreach is that it is to be done with people who are "different" from "us" in ways that invite or enable those people to become more like us.

At the heart of this value, centered on group identity, is the conviction that the individual must change to accommodate and support the needs and preferences of the group. Since the group has priority over the individual, and since it is the individual who ought to change to accommodate the group, differences can easily and directly be dealt with by determining the will or the direction of the majority. For this part of our congregations, *Robert's Rules of Order* and majority votes make perfect sense, as they are decision-making methods that quickly capture a picture of the will of the majority and simultaneously identify the individuals who should conform to the greater will of what is "right."

3. Assumptions of Sameness

Highly correlated with the marker of group identity is the value of sameness—an assumption that one size fits all. This idea conforms well with the group identity of the GI, "general issue," part of the congregation that learned its cultural lessons in a time of uniformity. I often ask groups to think back to 1940 and ask, if you wanted a telephone for your home back then, from how many models could you choose? People laugh and describe the standard model, the only phone available—black, heavy, with a rotary dial; attached to the wall by a sturdy cable. Now, to some extent, the selection of telephones was limited because the industry had not yet discovered computerization and digital and cellular technologies. Still, in the 1940s we did understand colors and shapes. Yet every phone was the same—black, boxy, and heavy.

This uniformity was acceptable because it fit the cultural assumption of sameness. If you needed a phone, you needed the same thing that everyone else needed in a phone. It was acceptable that they all be identical.

The same principle held true for congregations. It was assumed that if you needed a Lutheran or a Methodist congregation when you moved into a new community, you needed the same thing that other Lutherans or Methodists needed. Congregations were assumed, and expected, to come in "standard issue," and so you usually went to the closest local congregation of your denominational or faith tradition. Congregations and their leaders were measured and evaluated not on the basis of their unique effectiveness for the location or their appropriateness for the specific people they felt called to serve, but for their ability to be like other clergy and congregations of their tradition.

Congregations and their leaders were measured by a general standard, and the standard was one that could be generalized across the board. It made sense, then, to print an order of worship in the front of a denominational hymnal to be followed by all congregations of that denominational family each week at the regular service of worship. Uniformity was a standard of effectiveness. It made sense, then, to report to a denominational middle judicatory or national office using standardized report forms, or through formal reporting sessions with the denominational executive. A widely shared consensus prevailed as to what a congregation and its leaders should be doing. If all congregations were more or less the same, all reports on their practices could be filled out on identical forms. It was assumed that congregations were reporting on similar goals, using standard committee structures, and following standard financial practices.

In the language of management, the decisive question for congregations in the time of the GI culture was "Are we doing things right?" The measurement was then appropriately taken as leaders looked around them, across the landscape of neighboring congregations. Leaders could ask, "Does my congregation offer a Lenten Bible study series like other congregations of my denomination?" or "Do we participate in an Easter sunrise service like others?" or "Do we also have an annual women's bazaar to support foreign missions?"

The marker of conformity still holds great value for the GI-generation portion of our congregations. This committed portion of our leadership still asks the standard management question of whether we are doing things "right." Doing things right was once a measure taken horizontally by leaders looking across the congregational landscape at similar neighboring congregations. Was our congregation doing things the same way as everyone else? Today, however, the landscape is becoming more varied and confusing. It's harder to ask management questions about "doing things right." Today the measure is often taken by this long-tenured portion of the leadership and membership by looking not horizontally but historically, to ask if we are doing whatever is being measured exactly as we did it in the past.

One challenge for current leaders in congregations is to help everyone see that the use of past practices as a point of evaluation is not simply a matter of older members who are stuck in the past and unwilling to change. Indeed, in many cases, older people in our culture and our congregations are leading change. A large number of people over 65 are active participants and shapers of the Internet—because they have the time and the interest. An increasing number of people use retirement and later life for spiritual experimentation and deepening. Many older people have found opportunities that allow them to explore in new ways. These members of our congregations are not by definition rigid and unyielding. They are, however, people schooled in life lessons and in a value system that underscores continuity and asks evaluative questions to determine whether we are doing things right—often meaning the way that has proved effective in the past.

4. Spirituality of Place

Robert Wuthnow, professor of sociology at Princeton University, distinguishes between the established spirituality of dwelling and the spirituality of seeking. One is located in a place, the other in the journey. He writes:

> In settled times, people have been able to create a sacred habitat and to practice habitual forms of spirituality; in unsettled times, they have been forced to negotiate with themselves and with each other to find the sacred. Settled times have been conducive to an imagery of dwellings; unsettled times to an imagery of journeys. In one, the sacred is fixed, and spirituality can be found within the gathered body of God's people; in the other, the sacred is fluid, portable.[3]

For the people of Israel the difference was between the settled time of the Temple and the wandering time of the tabernacle.

The generational cohorts of the GI value system are oriented to the settled time, to a spirituality of place. The sacred can be found in a place to which one can go. Wuthnow notes that a spirituality of place "requires sharp symbolic boundaries to protect sacred space from its surroundings."[4] The boundaries may be physical, behavioral, or relational. Clearly, physical boundary issues were a concern for the pastor who tried to negotiate a compromise to allow the drums to stay permanently in the chancel area for use in the contemporary worship service. But no compromise could be found to accommodate what GI value carriers regarded as secular drums in a sacred space. In the GI value system, locating the sacred in a place of spirituality reinforces the idea that the church or synagogue requires different norms or behaviors. People who hold this value system appreciate hushed voices in the sanctuary, more formal dress and behavior, and careful attention to physical order (with a place for everything and everything in its place).

I well remember and appreciate the man in his 80s who participated in a group interview that I conducted in a large Lutheran church in Minnesota. We were seated in a circle of chairs in a contemporary worship space—a marvelous auditorium designed specifically for contemporary worship. With deep concern for his congregation, this man began to catalogue all that was wrong with the goings-on in this contemporary space. Because there were tables in the worship space, families could sit together around a table during worship. This arrangement led to inappropriate behavior, such as children coloring with crayons while the minister preached. Worse, some people's backs were turned to the altar when the communion elements were consecrated. The atmosphere also encouraged people to bring cups of coffee into the worship setting. And, the octogenarian concluded, obviously saving the most damning evidence for last, "they also bring those plastic water bottles that you can't get away from anywhere."

A spirituality of place has a settled nature that encourages tradition. Many homes, my own included, display the same holiday decorations in the same assigned place year after year. Once the Hanukkah candles or Christmas decorations are placed in an appropriate location, they reappear in that same place annually. As with seasonal decorations, so with seasonal practices. I grew up in a congregation that unfailingly sang Jean Baptiste Fauré's "The Palms" every year on Palm Sunday. Today I still leave my current congregation feeling disappointed on a Palm Sunday when we haven't sung this "old chestnut."

A spirituality of place easily establishes traditions of dress and behavior as well. From the GI generation's perspective, the acolyte who allows her sneakers to peek out from beneath her robe has allowed secular clothing and behavior to cross inappropriately into sacred space. (It does not matter that her sneakers may be her "best" and most expensive shoes.) For the GI generation, slightly bawdy jokes or occasionally spicy language allowed at the shopping mall or in the congregation's parking lot is disallowed once the threshold of sacred place has been crossed. To others who do not carry the GI value system, these distinctions may seem duplicitous or hypocritical. To those who live within this value system, they may simply seem faithful.

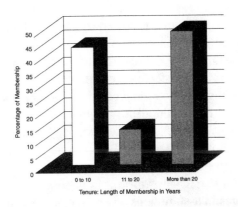

The Consumer Generation Value System

When we turn our attention to the short-tenured portion of the congregation, we may find a quite different, and often oppositional, value system undergirding people's assumptions, attitudes, and behaviors. Once again our description will be simplified and stereotypical. Once again, the goal is to describe cultural life lessons, not to establish or mark these values as right or wrong, better or worse than other values or value systems. Rather, these are the values learned and practiced because a group of people was born in a certain era and learned about life from the environment they encountered.

1. Instant Gratification

Where the GI value system honored and practiced deferred pleasure with its attendant disciplines and required patience, children of the consumer value system learned the lessons of instant gratification. Yankelovich quotes sociologist Daniel Bell as saying:

> The Protestant ethic was undermined by capitalism itself. The single greatest engine in the destruction of the Protestant ethic was the invention of the installment plan, or instant credit. Previously one had to save in order to buy. But with credit cards one could indulge in instant gratification.[5]

Surely the advent of instant credit was part of a much larger and more complex matrix of changes that followed World War II. Nonetheless, the postwar economy emphasized production. Many people were weary of deferring pleasures through a depression and a major war and were now itching to "catch up." These factors account for the shift in life lessons absorbed by the younger generational cohorts. The lessons no longer centered on saving until one could afford to buy a car or a refrigerator. The new cultural penchant was reflected in advertising slogans that encouraged purchasers to "buy now and pay later."

This cultural value shift is discussed at some length in the Alban Institute video "Living into the New World."[6] In that video I point to the many examples of changes in assumptions and behaviors that shaped the "now" generation that came of age in the 1960s, the "me" generation of the '70s and the "greed" generation of the '80s. These changing values and their life lessons form a remarkable story when viewed as part of a big picture, and looking at them as a cultural pattern aids our understanding of our national and congregational experience over recent decades. These changing cultural values have a major impact on the ministry of congregations and faith communities that live in the "new world" of consumerism. But the overwhelming effect of the cultural value shift that came on the heels of World War II was to teach people to expect not to wait.

The rise of instant credit taught people that they could take their goods home immediately and pay for them later. McDonald's (and the fast-food industry spawned from its example) told people that they could get their food almost instantly—food that was cheap and good. A drug industry began to produce medications and supplements that could reduce or eliminate symptoms almost immediately, and even people with chronic illnesses went in search of doctors and medicines that could provide the "silver bullet" that would solve the problem simply and quickly. People earned money but spent it immediately. For the first time in modern economics, concern arose over the paucity of voluntary financial savings practiced by Americans in comparison to people in other countries. Out of concern for the long-term security of the American people, who seemed to pay little attention to the long view, the federal government began a retirement savings program in IRAs (individual retirement accounts), in which the money could not be used until retirement. But to appeal to the consumer mentality, immediate tax relief was offered to savers in the same year that they contributed to their account. Some wonder if the IRAs would have held any attraction at all for age cohorts that expected immediate gratification, had an instant advantage not been attached to its use.

While the GI cultural value of deferred pleasure spoke *the language of responsibility,* the cultural values of the consumer generations spoke the *language of need.* One's value and one's place in the community were not measured so much by one's sense of responsibility and dependability as by one's sensitivity to self and one's ability to consume. To be a practiced consumer required a heightened sense of need—of knowing what one needed and wanted, and how to get it from the marketplace.

The highly sophisticated and accurate national marketing system was briefly described in chapter 1. Note the manner in which marketers have learned to observe and study each individual in our communities to give people access to whatever they think they need whenever they need it. In the process, the media and advertising industries have worked effectively together to help "teach people their needs" or to create a sense of need for specific products and services. Boomers and later generational cohorts have been thoroughly schooled in life lessons in consumption—lessons based on a language of need and a highly developed sense of uniqueness.

2. Individual Orientation

Whereas the GI value system found its identity in the group, the consumer value system focuses on the individual. Suddenly one is no longer expected to conform to group norms and practices; the individual is responsible for his or her own norms and practices based on a clear sense of one's own needs and "style." It is instructive to turn to the logos, mottoes, or sayings of the times that captured the moment. The GI value system emerged from generations that had been taught to "grin and bear it." The newer generations were taught quite different lessons. When it no longer sufficed for McDonald's to be fast, Burger King stepped in with its famous difference—"Have it your way"—and the importance of the individual was underscored. In the pivotal decade of the '60s the youth movement reminded people, "Don't trust anyone over 30" (since people over 30 had the wrong value system for these young learners of new cultural lessons), and "If it feels right, do it," perhaps the ultimate slogan of individualism in which the final arbiter of right or wrong is the individual with his or her own feelings. Beer companies pointed out the sobering truth that "you only go around once" and advised beer-drinkers to "grab all the gusto" while they could. Marketers of hair coloring conceded that their product was expensive, portraying young women with thick, shining tresses who concluded, "But I'm worth it."

Where once the culture was marked by deferred pleasure and assumptions of conformity, now immediacy and nonconformity held sway; and congregations, like schools, stores, banks, and an expanding array of service providers, were expected to identify and respond to individual needs. No longer did the individual conform to the group. Now the individual was to be elevated and served. Once it was sufficient to have a common-garden-variety credit card; now credit cards are individualized and customized with different interest rates, credit limits tailored to an individual's payment history, incentives that tie frequent-flyer miles to an airline of the user's choice, and even one's choice of art work on the laminated surface. Is it any wonder that congregations today find it necessary to clarify and claim a unique identity to fit a niche in communities and cultures finely tuned to the differences of individuals?

Once people assumed that a "right" way to worship should fit everyone in the group; now individuals go shopping for a worship style that best speaks to their preferences. Once consensus prevailed on the "right" way to build a budget and on the expectation that everyone would contribute a "fair share"; now finance committees look for ways to allow participants to designate their giving to a certain part of the budget, a particular program, or a favored mission project. Once voting was the accepted way to measure the level of consensus and to decide the direction in which the majority would lead the congregation. Today voting and *Robert's Rules of Order* are tools that capture our differences and spark competition—often creating conflict rather than resolving differences. In the wake of these changes in cultural teachings, congregational life is simply not the same.

3. Assumptions of Difference

Where the focus of the GI value system was on sameness, the focus of the consumer value system is clearly on difference. I already noted the high correlation between a group identity and assumptions about uniformity. If the individual is assumed to conform to the group, it is relatively easy to behave as though one size fits all (or that one size *should* fit all). If only one type of telephone was available for those who wanted one in 1946, consider how many types of telephones consumers can choose from today—or how many telephone service providers are available, each of which is more than willing to talk with you by phone about their service during your evening meal.

In an earlier time, if you were a Lutheran or a Methodist just arriving in town, you went in search of the nearest Lutheran or Methodist church with some assurance that it would serve you well because it was like other Lutheran or Methodist churches. Today you shop for the church that best fits your own needs (individualism) for this stage of your life (instant gratification). And it is OK for you to try out different brands. If you were a Lutheran in your last community, it is acceptable to visit the Assembly of God, the Episcopal parish, and the Baptist church in your new town to see which has the schedule, the atmosphere, the music, the programs, and the friendly members that best match your needs or preferences. This approach may make you suspect that religion is being reduced to consumerism and marketing—and that risk is present. But such a search also grows out of people's sensitivity and ability to know what life questions and spiritual questions they want to ask and their willingness to go looking for a place where their questions can be addressed.

Congregational leaders can no longer assume that they are doing things right just by doing what they have always done or by doing what other congregations in their denominational family do. Now leaders have to practice discernment and ask the more difficult questions about what their own congregation is called to do, to practice, or to provide because of its distinctive setting in the community among its special constituency, using its particular gifts. Today two Lutheran churches located across the street from each other (a not uncommon occurrence because of historical events) can expect to be quite unlike one another because each has distinctive gifts and is doing ministry with different people in a time when differences count.

4. Spirituality of Journey

As noted earlier, sociologist Robert Wuthnow has observed that the two sides of the generational watershed hold different assumptions about spirituality. "In one (the spirituality of place) the sacred is fixed, and spirituality can be found within the gathered body of God's people; in the other (the spirituality of journey) the sacred is fluid, portable." Each value system looks to encounter the sacred in a different place.

A parallel difference: In the GI value system, if a person is displeased or dissatisfied, the learned response is to dig in deeper, organize, work tenaciously, and fix what's wrong. In the consumer value system individual differences are the measure of satisfaction. If something displeases or does not satisfy, one simply *moves on.* This lesson of choice and freedom to seek is a life lesson of the marketplace to address the diverse needs of its customers. When the consumer is roaming the shopping mall looking for black slacks and discovers that the store she's in has none that fit, she doesn't organize with others to make her displeasure known or to try to change the store. The shopper just moves on to the next clothing store to see if what she needs can be found there.

Similarly, the spiritual journey or quest simply continues. Those who pursue the spirituality of journey do not necessarily identify a special place as important in the encounter with God. People on a pilgrimage are willing to search and to encounter God in both likely and unlikely places; they are ready to move about to find God. This search can confuse the holders of GI values, who associate spirituality with place. The pursuit can lead to "multiple memberships" for those responding to consumer values. They may "belong" to one congregation because they prefer the style of worship there, but simultaneously "belong" to another congregation for the youth program, while also "belonging" to a third congregation because of a helpful support group or study course. In all of these "memberships," the carrier of consumer values may never take the formal step of officially joining the congregation but may be satisfied that participation is "belonging" enough. For an adherent of the GI value system, with its focus on the importance of the group and of belonging, the portable spirituality of the consumer group is confounding and displeasing. This intergenerational discomfort is further exacerbated when encounters with the spiritual for some in the consumer value group also include practices outside their own tradition such as yoga, Tai Chi, or 12-step programs.

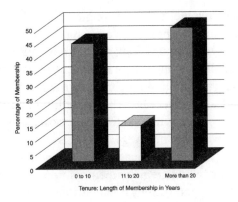

Tenure: Length of Membership in Years

The Bridge People

At the beginning of this chapter I identified a third subgroup that has a separate character in the congregation. This usually smaller group of members resides in the middle between the larger clusters of GI value carriers and consumer value carriers. These really are people in the middle. As noted in the bimodal distribution model, they have commonly been members of the congregation from 10 to 20 years. They come with their own life lessons from one side of the 1946 watershed or the other, with preferences for the GI or the consumer value system. But functioning within the congregational system, they tend to be sensitive to and understanding of both large clusters.

No matter how long-tenured the clergy and program staff of the congregation may be (newly arrived or 20-year veterans), they nonetheless, as staff, live their lives in the congregation as part of this bridge group, in the middle. They are expected to understand and to represent both divergent value systems. They are expected to bridge the differences and make the sense of community "work" for everyone.

Bridge people are expected to be multilingual, able to speak the languages and respond to the markers of both value systems that flank them. Because they stand in the middle and understand both languages, they are often looked upon as problem solvers, as people who are responsible to negotiate with the "other side" to make it work.

One difficulty often encountered by bridge people is the perception that they are "siding with" the newer members who represent consumer values. This reaction is a natural but difficult consequence of the misunderstandings of behavior dividing the congregation's two dominant value systems.

It is common in many established congregations for the GI value cohort to have a much more expressive voice in decision making. After all, these members have been around longer and know the norms better. But more than that, their life lessons encourage them to organize to make their preferences known. They willingly defer their needs and pleasures to devise strategies to get what they want. They're willing to work and wait for their views to prevail. Theirs is usually the voice most clearly heard at board meetings and congregational meetings. Theirs is the opinion most easily registered by surveys of the congregation that often get the best responses from people who know how to register their opinion.

In contrast, many congregations find it difficult to hear and understand the voice of newer participants who carry the consumer values of immediacy, individuality, difference, and journey. These newer members do not necessarily see themselves as a group and don't organize to get their needs and preferences heard. They often don't assume that others need or want what they are looking for. The portability of their search means that if they don't find what they are looking for in one congregation, they can rather easily leave and move on to the next congregation to see if the fit is better. Often the first hint congregational leaders detect to indicate that members of this group are displeased or unsatisfied comes from noticing that they have been absent.

In such a situation behaviors consistent with the values of the two groups give the longer-tenured members a more dominant voice. Realizing the importance of having the voices of short-tenured people heard, the bridge group quite naturally steps in to protect and to give a platform to the quieter and sometimes diffident voices of the short-tenured members who carry consumer values.

For the bridge people, representing the short-tenured members and attenders is often seen as a matter of fairness. For staff and key lay leaders, this act is often regarded as a critical issue of listening to the voice of the "future" that speaks too quietly and needs to be heard. But not surprisingly, for the long-tenured GI-value-centered members, this representation of the short-tenured people is often perceived as a betrayal. The bridge people suffer under this assumption. The GI value holders are not mean-spirited. Rather, they make different assumptions about their group identity, for they are people who value the group and their membership in the group. For them, if someone is not standing with them (in their group), that person must be standing against them (favoring some other group). When bridge people, especially clergy, program staff, and key laypeople, stand with the newer members to help their quieter voices be heard or interpreted, the long-tenured members (who still assume that, given enough time, even the new members will become more like them) can feel betrayed.

The experience of living and leading from the bridge position is draining and often uncomfortable. "Multilingual" people needing to speak both of the "languages" of the competing value systems find that they can tire quickly and become depleted from a lack of appreciation from either side. The difficulty of this bridge position and the personal toll that it can take was put into words by an active member of a congregation with which I was consulting. We had been working on differences in expectations between these two cultural value groups, and one point of discomfort had expressed itself in worship. Members were having a difficult debate about whether applause in worship was appropriate. The longer-tenured folk, with their value on the spirituality of place, were uncomfortable that community behavior, such as applause appropriate to a performance, was creeping over the boundary into their sacred space. The shorter-tenured people, with their value on immediacy and individuality, were eager to have a place where they could participate, and did not see worship as a performance but as a venue to express themselves in their own search. The lines were drawn, and the conversation had been strained. The real burden on the bridge people was given voice by a man in his late 40s who had been an active member for about 12 years. He said that when the children's choir finished singing, he was one of those who applauded. He did so because he appreciated what the singers had put into their music; he wanted them to feel that they had a place in this congregation and that the members could accept them and meet their needs. But, the man continued, every time he clapped, he felt both sad and guilty—because he knew that he was breaking the heart of his father, who was standing next to him.

Not for the Faint of Heart

Many established congregations have a daily life and rhythm determined by the cultural value differences held by their members. I have sat in competitive hymn sings in which long-tenured members called out the names of "old chestnut" hymns for the whole group to sing and short-tenured members responded with names of contemporary praise songs or the newest "global" hymns from the denominational hymnal. The energy of the group was high, but it was hard to tell whether the people really wanted to sing the hymns they named or whether they wanted to force others to sing the very songs those others would not have selected. In congregational listening groups I have heard long-tenured members complain that newer members would not join committees and serve on the board, while newer members complained that they were not permitted to participate in decision making—and both were right.

Leading and living in a multigenerational congregation is not for the faint of heart. But the experience can occasion rich and dynamic conversation about the presence of God in our lives, the fabric of faith, and negotiations for the values and truths that will be passed to the next generation. Often approached too seriously and in a win/lose spirit, this wonderful conversation needs to be held a bit more lightly and treated with more enjoyment and delight. That conversation is what you are invited to join in chapter 6, as we begin to explore the way in which differences are lived out in the congregation.

CHAPTER 5

Biblical Glimpses: Part II

Connecting the daily work of decision making to the faith it represents is the task of spiritual leadership. In this second example of connecting with the biblical story, an Episcopal vestry was fully aware of its own discomfort but was unsure of the cause. The priest asked me to spend a day with the vestry to explore why an argument erupted in the group every year. The vestry members were a friendly group; they firmly supported their priest, and they had a high regard for the church's worship life and programs, one fully shared by leaders and members alike.

This parish and its leadership seemed healthy and vibrant. Yet each year a dispute over goals broke out within the vestry, lasting from November to February. Since budget-building time fell within these months, everyone acknowledged that money was somehow a factor in the discomfort. The congregation lived within a reasonable budget and had a few small reserved funds. But it needed to budget carefully and set priorities because resources were limited. Each year it seemed more difficult to balance the budget. Except for wrestling over what new programs or projects would be supported by the next year's budget, it was a well-functioning governing board in a vibrant congregation. Vestry members were bothered that their meetings could be expected to bog down annually in acrimonious debates over the shaping of the next year's budget.

Late in the morning of our day's work I gave a small group of vestry members the task of finding their biblical story. Two other small groups of leaders were given two separate tasks, and all three groups were asked to report back to the full group after lunch. As we were finishing lunch, the biblical-story group members came to me to report that they didn't know what I had planned for early afternoon, but that they were going first! They had found their story.

These leaders reported that they had discovered the story of Jesus' visit to Martha and Mary (Luke 10:38-42). They were sure that this story explained what their dispute was about. They then recounted the story for the full group, telling how Mary sat at the feet of Jesus and listened while Martha took care of the guests. According to the text, Martha, upset with her role, "was distracted by her many tasks; so she came to him and asked, 'Lord, do you not care that my sister has left me to do all the work by myself?'"

"That's what we do," explained the small-group leader. The group explained that every year at budget time the vestry argued over which role was more important, Mary's or Martha's. They would battle over the extra money that they squeezed into the budget, over whether it was more important to move ahead on the project to put protective storm windows over the sanctuary's stained glass (Martha's role), or to sponsor another mission trip to South America like those that had provided a spiritual boost to a number of members (Mary's role). "That's us," concluded the woman presenting the report. "Some of us are always worried about doing the dishes while others just want to go sit and talk to Jesus."

As they explored the story, vestry members began to find their own place in the narrative. To everyone's surprise the Martha role, with concern for the storm windows, was overwhelmingly supported by the long-tenured GI value system representatives and championed most effectively by the long-tenured treasurer, who was influential in the budgeting process. The mission trip and support of new programs for spiritual exploration, Mary's role, were taken up by the short-tenured board members who most frequently felt underrepresented and defensive. The result was an annual battle instead of an open dialogue.

Using the biblical story, vestry members concluded that they needed to learn how to listen more sensitively to both Martha and Mary. They challenged themselves in the following year to establish a dual agenda for each board meeting in which they would allot at least 20 minutes to "Mary" and 20 minutes to "Martha," along with other operational business items that needed to be addressed. They were committing themselves to listen and learn across their bimodal differences in ways that would balance and complete their lives as a faith community.

CHAPTER 6

Living in the New Congregation

When my wife and I were preparing to be married, our minister handed us a book to read as part of our premarital preparation. The author of that book pointed out that we would learn that even in the simplest situations, we would make use of our separate backgrounds and lessons, and play different roles that would make us see clear realities in distinctive ways. We still refer to the example the author used: When asked, "Where did you get the steak?" the husband might answer, "At the grocery store." But when asked the same question, the wife might respond, "Why? What's wrong with it?"

Even at that time, we thought that the example was a bit stereotyped and sexist, perhaps playing too much into marital roles we were not sure we would follow. But our discomfort with the example did not stop us from recognizing that the writer was correct about differences. We often found ourselves experiencing a conversation or event and responding with different if not opposite thoughts and feelings. Over the lifetime of a marriage these contrasting responses make for good stories and fond memories. However, such differences have sometimes felt like pinch points and made us squirm.

To an extent, the steak story is a parable of life in a multigenerational system. People can hear the same words but receive different messages. People sitting side by side can witness the same incident and come away with diametrically opposed feelings or understandings. A leader can ask a question and receive opposing responses from different quarters of the congregation, with each side surprised by the other's views.

People in multigenerational and bimodal congregations have fundamentally positive feelings toward each other, enjoy being with each other, and often seek each other out. As discussed in chapter 2, each of these groups consciously or intuitively understands that the other part of the congregation holds some value or offers a difference that contributes to a completeness that they cannot supply themselves. Long-term members of the congregation see energy, potential, and youth in the shorter-tenured members. In these newer members is the promise that the faith and this valued congregation will continue and prosper. Similarly, short-tenured members seek out longer-tenured members, most of whom are older than they. The longer-tenured members represent resident wisdom and an opportunity to reflect on life experience that is not commonly available around multigenerational kitchen tables in a highly mobile society. This longer-tenured membership core also represents security and resources for the congregation, which is valued by all as a place to be preserved.

However, to the confusion of many, and to the consternation of leaders, these groups of people who value each other, choose to be with one another, and even actively seek each other out, do not communicate well with one another. Often using exactly the same words, they can deliver unmatching, even opposite messages. Committed to the same values, they can make decisions that absolutely deny the need of the other. The varying generational value systems are the cause of this confusion. Revealing the distinctions of value systems is crucial to learning to live with the dissonance. But since congregations are more sensitive to behaviors than to ideas, they learn better from stories than from theory. It is necessary to unpack the ideological and value-laden features of each generational value structure, using the stories of real people in real congregations. In this chapter, we will go inside the daily life of a faith community and witness the bimodal congregation in its frustrating but healthy complexity.

Finances and Reserved Funds

An observer might begin with any number of subjects, but I will turn to one of my favorites—money. Can you imagine that people of a common faith can use shared language with identical intent and still come out thinking that the "other side" is wasteful and wrong? Easy. All you need do is attend a committee meeting about the use of reserved funds.

Many congregations hold assets beyond the funds needed for the current budget, and they must decide how to manage or to spend these dollars. In the present environment, in the midst of a massive transfer of wealth from one generation to another, it is not uncommon that congregations receive bequests or gifts of nonbudget revenue or real property. In these cases some individual or group must determine the use or management of these assets. Often a committee is formed or a congregational meeting called to decide, "What shall we do with this additional asset?"

Let's create a scenario that is common to many bimodal congregations. Upon receipt of a bequest, or the word of a bequest, a committee is formed to decide what to do with this fresh asset. To exercise inclusion and fairness, the committee commonly balances new and old members, younger and older people. If the committee already exists, as it does in many larger congregations, its makeup still generally includes this mix of members. Leaders want people to be represented, their viewpoints heard, and their sense of belonging and voice supported. In many congregations then, the committee is guaranteed to represent the fundamental differences of the competing value systems found in bimodal congregations. With full agreement, committee members will use the same question and agree on the same language to shape the agenda for their task: How shall we be faithful stewards of this new asset?

With common purpose and language, they will frustrate one another with their competing conclusions. "Save," some will say. "Spend," others will insist. Leaders cannot miss the point that both conclusions are reasonable and appropriate responses to the agreed-upon question.

Once again, this conflict is the product of the life lessons of different generational cohorts. When I ask groups the dominant response of the GI value system to extra assets, the answer is unfailingly "Save it!" Two rules for reserved funds prevail among the GI generation. Rule 1: The money must be saved for a rainy day. Rule 2: It never rains.

When I worked with leaders in one congregation, we took a break after talking about this generation's response to reserved funds, and a pastor came up to me for private conversation. He told me that his congregation's sanctuary had caught fire, resulting in about $400,000 worth of damage. The insurance coverage for the damage would pay for about $300,000 of the repairs and rebuilding, and the congregation had about $900,000 in reserved funds. He and several members of the church assumed that the reserved funds could make up the difference between the cost of repairs and the insurance payment—only to be told that the money was unavailable because the church was "saving it for a rainy day." The pastor noted that his greatest surprise was realizing "how hard it had to rain" before people felt that they could touch those invested assets that made them feel secure.

The GI value system is not punitive, and the people are not necessarily tight with money. A value system is strongly shaped by life lessons, and the GI cohort experienced insecurity and the need to defer pleasure in the Great Depression and the Second World War. During the Depression, the life lesson for many people was uncertainty that they would have the assets needed for security; they could not be confident that they would have tomorrow the assets they had today. Under those conditions, good congregational management and faithful stewardship meant protecting existing funds and not using them unless confronted with dire circumstances that could not be managed any other way. Stability in an insecure environment meant protecting assets.

The need for sacrifice was another lesson of the Second World War, and people learned to live with government-imposed rationing. Purchases and pleasures were deferred for the good of the nation. The lesson learned, and learned well, by this cohort was one of sacrifice and deferred pleasure. Save.

It should not surprise us that the people who hold this value system in the present-day congregation respond the same way. When a congregation must make decisions about managing reserved funds to underwrite its future, this part of the membership will easily choose to protect and preserve this meaningful institution by saving the extra assets and protecting them from being spent. Safeguarding such assets is, from the perspective of this value system, protecting the future of the congregation itself.

But where one voice says save, the other voice says spend. Here the cohort of newer members often enters into conversations about the appropriate stewardship of reserved funds or bequests by considering how the money might be used immediately.

When I ask congregational leaders to identify how newer members commonly suggest spending extra dollars not needed to support annual budget needs, I hear several basic categories of responses:

- Technology such as computers, Internet Web page development, e-mail systems, sound systems, and projection systems for worship;
- Facility improvement, such as general upgrading for a welcoming appearance or renovating areas such as child-care space;
- Mission experiences that will involve members of the congregation in a hands-on project; and
- Spiritual development programming or support-group development.

Characteristically, longer-tenured members will add comments during these conversations, such as "they spend it all on themselves," as if the willingness to spend reserved funds were somehow selfish and self-centered. However, for short-tenured members, the issue is not self-service or impulsiveness, but rather the identical question that the longer tenured members are seeking to address: faithful stewardship of the assets of their congregation. However, instead of moving toward saving or security, the shorter-tenured participants, because of their value system, lean toward utility and active use of resources. They think in terms of facilities, resources, or activities to attract and encourage participation of people of the post-GI culture. For shorter-tenured members, money is less universally viewed as equivalent to security. It is perceived, instead, as a tool that can be used to achieve identified goals.

The life lesson of this newer consumer cohort is quite different from that of the GIs. This group of people grew up in a constantly expanding economy where consumers were encouraged to spend their dollars today, and it was assumed that there would always be more dollars tomorrow. This group also grew up in an inflationary economy in which it was advisable to use your dollar today for purchase or investment, because that dollar would be worth less tomorrow. What is the appropriate action and evidence of good stewardship in such a situation? It is to be open to the possibility of spending as a way of capitalizing on one's resources for the future.

These two groups with their divergent value systems want to talk about "faithful stewardship" of resources. Both groups believe that they are in agreement and working together—until one side defines stewardship as saving and the other defines it as spending. Suddenly, the large cultural differences emerge, and collaborative understanding breaks down.

Talking to a group of congregational leaders about the bimodal congregation, a pastor offered a classic example of this value-driven difference in how money is regarded. His congregation, having recently received a sizable bequest, formed a task force to decide on its use. Like many other task forces, this one by design included both newer and longer-term leaders. After months of disagreement on the use of the bequest, the pastor began one meeting by provoking a more creative response. Placing a stack of silver half-dollars in the middle of the boardroom table, he invited the task force members not to explain what should be done with the bequest but to use the half-dollars to *show* others what to do. The first to respond, one of the longest-tenured task-force members, took the half-dollars, placed them in a neat stack in front of him on the table, firmly placed his open palm on top of the stack, and said, "That's what you do with the money. You protect it." As he pushed the money back to the center of the table, the group fell silent for a moment or two. The next to move was one of the church's newest members, who reached out and took only one half-dollar. Setting it on its edge on the table with one hand, he flicked the side of the coin with a finger of his other hand and sent the coin skating across the table spinning like a top. "That's what you do with the money," said the newer member. "You make it move."

Leaders and members of bimodal congregations often need to learn how not to see opponents sitting across the table from them. Instead a participant needs to learn how to see the different life lessons guiding others who seek to address the same questions—life lessons that lead to conclusions other than the ones that the watching participant might naturally consider.

If encountering this disagreement is difficult for participants, it is clearly exasperating for leaders who have the responsibility for helping the group reach a decision. Differences based on value systems easily break down to a search for winners and losers. Although it might seem reasonable in the present example to invest or save a portion of the bequest, while spending a portion, commonly leaders discover little room for satisfying compromise. Such a situation can be seen in the next example.

Women's Circles and Support Groups

Congregations across a broad range of denominations and faith traditions have established women's circles, women's societies, women's boards, or sisterhoods as a historic part of their organizational structure. In many congregations these circles or societies are shrinking in size and energy, despite the presence of a sizable, even growing number of younger, newer women in the congregation.

A common tale in congregations I have visited: The established women's organization has become increasingly aware of its diminished size and strength as it tries to manage its annual schedule of activities and events. Looking around at the other women in the congregation, the circle officers reach out to them, either by personal conversation or by formal invitation. Often the circle leaders take extra steps to provide a welcoming entry point by hosting a get-acquainted tea or providing a special program or event to introduce prospective members to their group.

Often the results are dismal. Few newer women respond, or a positive response to an initial tea is followed by a dramatic drop of interest in subsequent meetings. The poor response often prompts critical remarks from each side. Circle members comment that the newer women are too self-involved to think of others, and younger prospects note that the longer-tenured women of the circles maintain a different lifestyle that allows for afternoon circle meetings, precluding participation by employed women and those with major family responsibilities. The remarks of both the women who invite and the women invited often contain elements of truth and criticism. What the women commonly fail to address is the difference in value systems and life lessons that make this area of congregational life a stand-off between two groups of women that appreciate each other.

Approached from the perspective of life lessons, women's organizations in congregations are historically important places for many women of the GI value system. In an earlier North American society that was uncritically male-dominated, few places outside congregations offered opportunities for women's leadership and leadership development.

Women were not invited to be decision makers and organizers in business or public organizations. Few opportunities were available for them to practice entrepreneurial activities. In such a situation women turned to their congregations as a common place where they could legitimately gather and organize their own activities, set their own goals to accomplish work of importance, practice leadership, and provide leadership development for younger women. This last purpose was particularly clear in one congregation I worked with, in which the women's organization had historically elected younger members to officers' positions and assigned older, more experienced women as mentors to work with them on planning and leading meetings.

For women who lived with the life lessons and generational values of the GI cohort, congregations became the prime place to identify important goals and to exercise with purpose their values of group life and deferred pleasure. Afternoon teas or coffee klatches made sense as a means of developing group identity.

Purposeful activities were the norm. Medical supplies and blankets were gathered and sent to mission fields. Missionaries were identified, and support links were developed for prayer and financial support, communications, and occasional stateside visits. Artwork and artifacts from Japan, China, Africa, and South America would show up in local congregations as cross-cultural studies were undertaken to deepen relationships with mission projects in other countries, as well as to educate and challenge members of the congregation. Holiday bazaars, fairs, and strawberry festivals were organized. Craft and baked-goods sales raised dollars to provide mission support, upgrade the congregation's facilities, or help pay off the mortgage on a new property.

In many congregations the women's organization was a prime vehicle through which the congregation carried out its local charity work, provided international mission support, and raised funds for congregational development above and beyond the annual expense budget. Weekly gatherings for handicraft work, sewing groups, and the management of neighborhood clothing centers or food programs were highly organized and effective means of putting shared values and beliefs to work.

Leadership in the congregational women's organization became the doorway to larger venues and opportunities of leadership for women. Ecumenical and interfaith women's organizations also allowed women to also take their place in the larger community. Denominational women's organizations were appropriately hierarchical and bureaucratic in ways favored by the GI value system of organized group life. This denominational and ecumenical structure gave women from the local congregational setting a much larger landscape to practice their leadership at district, regional, state, and national levels. Many North American faith traditions and denominations still have powerful and influential national (or international) women's divisions that not only raise large dollar amounts and organize vast volunteer resources but also represent dominant voices of influence over policy and polity decisions.

Viewed from this perspective, the local congregation's women's circle was much more than an afternoon out for the women of the GI value system. It was an opportunity to participate in purposefulness beyond one's individual life and family setting, as well as a platform for leadership and leadership development. In fact, these organizations continue to offer women in the local congregation today this same opportunity for leadership and purposefulness.

This story is viewed quite differently, however, by people of the consumer-value perspective. Often missed is the point that, given the generational value shifts and cultural changes of recent decades, one of the *last* things many younger women want or need is *another* place to exercise purpose and leadership. The shift from deferred pleasure to instant gratification provided more opportunities for women to organize and move to the public sphere of community life, business, and politics. Support was offered to individual women to step forward in leadership without deferring to men or waiting for an invitation. The acronym of the National Organization for Women, NOW, clearly and appropriately symbolizes the shift away from deferred pleasure and announces the presence of women in national life. Gender discrimination was minimized by law and practice, and despite the "glass ceiling" that still effectively cordons women off from some levels or offices in organizations, women are sought after in businesses, professions, and public institutions.

For these women, leadership is no longer an opportunity to be sought after but rather an overwhelming expectation to be played out simultaneously in the family, the community, and one's career, as evidence of one's personal worth.

In the GI generational value system, it made perfect sense for women to meet weekly to knit woolen goods for the congregation's November holiday bazaar, hoping to raise $1,200 to support mission work or to supplement payments on the congregation's mortgage. The money was important, but it was only the most visible product of valuable opportunities for gathering, enjoying social support, developing group identity, pursuing organizational opportunities, and developing leadership skills.

However, in the experience of women shaped by the consumer-value system, the opportunities represented by the November holiday bazaar are redundant and, in fact, overwhelming when placed alongside the daunting expectations of a busy family life and a professional career. Weekly gatherings that cost time and effort cannot justify a $1,200 gain to be put toward a much larger mission or mortgage commitment. From the perspective of women born after 1945, writing a check could provide the same or more dollar support with much less effort and still allow time and energy to address life's other requirements.

Hence, women's organizations in congregations became another focus for miscommunication and misunderstanding between generations that speak the same language but with different meanings. Are women's groups important and needed? Women of both generational value systems would say yes—a response that suggests they are speaking the same language and voicing agreement. But when the GI generational cohort offers invitations for organizational membership, volunteer commitments, and leadership responsibilities, they feel offended and devalued by the consumer-value cohort that will not respond. The "yes" of the consumer cohort often means that they need or want a support group, a retreat experience, or a hands-on mission project where they can clearly see the difference their effort makes and feel a direct sense of connection. The consumer-value group feels diminished and offended when the GI-value group refers to them as uncommitted, selfish, or irresponsible.

Mission and Social Welfare Concerns

Similar confusion can be seen in other arenas of congregational life. Consider the concern for mission or social welfare outreach, which begins at the same point of apparent agreement and harmony across the generational divide. Members of most congregations, whatever their generation, agree that mission is important and that the church should reach out to help others less fortunate. But as the conversation moves toward financial or programmatic responses to that shared agreement, the tensions in bimodal congregations may erupt.

Consider the locus of influence. For people of the GI value system the primary target for mission or social welfare is the "other." With this cohort's emphasis on the importance of group and belonging, a primary goal for mission or welfare outreach is to change the "others" to help them become more like the group. In an earlier day, foreign mission efforts were organized not merely to share one's faith with the other but also to inculcate the other with one's language, educational standards, dress, and behavior. Not consciously seen as an imposition on the other, mission work was offered as an extension of a value system in which people wanted to share an important group identity and belonging. There was little focus on changing the self through missional efforts, since the self already belonged and was part of the group. Mission could therefore best be carried out by sending financial and material resources to distant locales to be managed by professional missionaries or social workers. To change the other, one had to go where the other was—which most often meant sending resources to inner-city areas, Appalachian poverty pockets, or world missions in Africa, India, or China. One could not do mission or outreach in one's own backyard, because the people nearby were most like one and were already a part of the group.

The shift in cultural value systems moved the critical emphasis from the group to the individual, and in so doing shifted the locus or target of mission and welfare from an exclusive focus on the other to a more intentional inclusion of the self. In this understanding, the purpose of missional outreach is no longer to make the other more like "us." Differences are now honored and protected. The purpose of missional and social outreach is to help change people, and in the minds of the people of the consumer value system, changing the self is as valuable as changing the other. This part of the congregation wants to engage in outreach in ways that change themselves as much as the other. Rather than sending dollars and material resources to professional missionaries, these people want to go on a mission trip to Belize to help build a school with their own hands, to meet a people of a different culture face to face, to get a different world perspective, and to experience their own beliefs and commitments in an environment that will help them reevaluate those beliefs and commitments back home. Building a school and helping the other are not incidental. But whereas people of the GI value system would send money to have the school built and to help change the indigenous people to be more like them, the people of the consumer-value system would encourage others to go to the site and pound the nails and meet the people so that the self will be challenged or changed in the process as well.

Is mission or social welfare outreach important, and should we commit a portion of our resources to meet the needs of others? When the question is asked in the bimodal congregation, the response is a unanimous yes, along with a willingness to move ahead voiced from all quarters. People think that they have consensus. That quick agreement and the assumption of a shared language about mission and welfare move swiftly to disputes. The question of where to direct our money reminds the bimodal congregation of its value differences. The people of the GI value system assume that the money will go directly to the denominational program through denominational channels as an agreed-upon way to introduce our faith to other people, who will be invited to become more like us. The people of the consumer value system will respond with questions: Why can't the money be used to send individuals from our own congregation to participate in a life-changing experience that will help others but also change them? Why can't these people come back to our own congregation after the trip to tell their stories and help change those of us who did not take the trip? Why can't the dollars be used for neighborhood mission or outreach projects to the children in the neighborhood, so that a parking-lot summer program can enable us to meet our immediate neighbors and to become more sensitive to the people in our midst who are different from us? Why can't we pick our own mission or outreach programs stemming from out own interests and commitments, no matter what the denomination recommends about using only its official channels? Once again, after agreeing on the topic to be explored, the two sides of the bimodal congregation quickly move into separate and unconnected conversations.

Membership and Belonging

Membership for people who hew to the GI value system means *belonging*. With the emphasis on group life, membership for these people focuses on being part of the group. Being a member is as much an issue of identity as it is of participation. In chapter 2, I recalled President Dwight Eisenhower's challenge in the 1950s for every American "to belong to a religion, some religion." It was a time in which one's specific beliefs were less important than being part of a group that had a set of beliefs. Belonging was an expression of one's identity. Who you were was tied closely to your group affiliations. Most people could point to "their" church or synagogue, even if they seldom or never participated in the worship, program, or group life.

For people of the GI value system, the alignment of "belonging" with identity brings special meaning to formal membership and to symbolic and sacramental acts such as baptism. Formal membership is important, because it is the boundary one must step over to be part of the group. Being "one of us," or "not one of us," is an issue of formal membership. Emphasis on confirmation or other rites or procedures of joining leads to paying stricter attention to which people can claim the rights and privileges of the group, such as voting at a congregational meeting, being elected an officer of the congregation, serving on some committees, or perhaps helping to count the collection after worship.

Within the Christian community, this sense of membership leads to the question often asked by parents and grandparents, to the annoyance of many priests and pastors—"When can we have the baby done?"—an obvious reference to the sacrament of baptism. The theological recognition of this infant as a child of God to be nurtured in the faith community is reduced almost to an issue of clan identity. Seen as the primary rite of initiation into both the family and the congregation, baptism is often viewed through this cultural lens as the crossing of a boundary to become officially "one of us." Formal congregational membership and baptismal membership are often markers for who is in and who is out, whom we call upon and whom we do not, who has influence and who does not.

The North American Protestant history of social-class mobility was once tied to this same sense of identity. Certain denominations, and in many communities particular congregations, represented different socioeconomic community groups. In many places as one moved from blue-collar to white-collar, from entry level to executive level, it was not uncommon for a family to move from one denominational group to another to underscore the change of reference groups in the community. In one small town, I consulted with a United Methodist congregation that was one of two churches of the same denomination less than four blocks apart. Historically, this was a mill town dominated by the local mill works. If one was a manager at the mill, he was expected to belong to the Methodist church for the managers. A laborer was expected to belong to the other. If one was promoted from labor to management, the promotion carried with it the tacit expectation that the worker would soon transfer his membership to the appropriate Methodist church.

For people of the consumer value system, membership carries a far more casual meaning. Membership is measured by the individual's *participation* rather than by identity. Do I continue to come back? Do I participate with regularity? Is what I do here meaningful? Attendance and participation are measures of the importance of the congregation to the individual; they don't need to be underwritten by formal vows of membership and do not depend on listing the constituent's name in the formal register of members. Membership is not a formal boundary to be crossed for inclusion in the group. Instead, a sense of belonging comes from the individual's intentional connection, reflecting the value discovered in the relationship.

These differences are subtle, but here we see another instance where a common vocabulary can lead to argument. When a congregational meeting for all "members" is called, people of the GI value system carefully count only the formal members whose names are on the official register. In controversial moments, efforts will be made to produce votes from formal members who long ago stopped participating and may not even understand the issue in question. Nonetheless, to the GI generation, they are "one of us" with vote and voice and an interest in who we are and where we are going. This strict interpretation of membership can offend the consumer-value portion of the congregation—some of whom are active and committed participants in the life of the congregation but don't feel the same need to seek formal membership. Deeply committed and active, they are astonished to find themselves without voice or vote at a critical moment.

The definition of membership as "participation" by adherents to the consumer value system can also be offensive to the GI value-system people who depend on identity. This discomfort leads to confusing behavior. Membership as participation allows for multiple memberships. In this case a mother might "belong" to one congregation for its strong worship program and its active mother's support group; "belong" to another congregation for its strong youth program, where her children willingly participate; and "belong" to a third congregation because of its outstanding Bible-study group. Proponents of the GI value system, with its emphasis on the group and on responsibility, are offended by what they interpret as disloyalty. Those shaped by the consumer-value system, with its emphasis on the individual and on individual needs, would not feel disloyal to any of the three congregations but rather feel a connection to and an appreciation for what was received from each of them.

One group I worked with, the 30-member program committee of an active congregation, was asking itself why the congregation was not growing as fast as the surrounding community. I was struck that this was a fairly sophisticated question for a program group. It indicated that the leaders had already compared their congregation's growth with that of its environment. I was doubly struck by committee members' language, once we got into the work, because they continually referred to their church as "not growing." When I pointed out the discrepancy—they had already measured the growth but still spoke of the church as not growing—they responded that, yes, there were more people in the church now but "they are not really good members." Laughing, because we all realized that they were caught in the trap of their own words, I stopped our work and asked the participants to describe a "good member." Not surprisingly, they described themselves— people of singular commitment to this one congregation, active in all of its parts, and willing to step over the formal line of membership to "sign on the dotted line." They were offended by the "members by participation" who did not live up to their standards of "membership by identity." But they were not aware that they equally offended the "members by participation" by devaluing them and making it harder for them to be included. Were one to ask the parties on both sides of this cultural value divide if belonging to this congregation was important to them, the answer would be a resounding "Yes!" But did they understand and communicate with one another well in ways that supported inclusion and community building? Not at all.

Committees and Organizational Structure

In leading groups to explore the bimodal congregations, I often ask which value-system cohort likes committees. The immediate response is always that it is the GI generation. A committee is a group experience. That observation does not suggest that we should immediately reject all committees as anachronistic, belonging only to the GI value system, or inappropriate to the present cultural direction. We still need organizational management that uses committees and some hierarchical structure. But it does help to see that an overdependence on committees and organizational structure is much more consistent with people who hold GI values than with those who have consumer values. Here again common language and needs lead quickly to significant differences in the bimodal congregation.

Parties on both sides of the cultural-value divide share a common language and a common concern that good leadership is important to the life and future of the congregation. But the GI cohort often is offended by newer members who won't accept nominations for committee membership, and the consumer cohort is equally offended by the longer-termed members who insistently urge them to join a committee, as if that's what new members were looking for when they found this congregation.

The focus of the GI value system on group life and deferred pleasure allows for the commitment of a good bit of time to decision making and planning. A high value is placed on developing agreement and moving ahead as a group. Multiple meetings to make and check decisions seem sensible from this perspective. To begin planning for a holiday program six months in advance, with monthly meetings and multiple checkpoints to ensure that all materials are ordered at lowest cost to be delivered on time, is a preferred way to operate. Levels of authority in which committees members need to check ideas and receive approvals from program boards, which in turn must check plans with the governing board, are understandable components of an organizational system built on consensus and a group awareness in which individuals and their preferences must be blended to accommodate the group.

Such organizational life depends upon a large number of volunteers to manage two group principles—cohesion and representation. Doing this work well allows the congregation to move ahead collaboratively and provides a good sense of inclusion for all participants.

The consumer-value system, however, operates with a different sensitivity and time line which does not favor redundant decision-making processes and does not value cohesion and representation as highly. The more action-oriented people of the consumer-value system prefer decisions to be made and responsibility managed closer to the action—for example, at the committee or task force level. Approvals by multiple levels of the congregational hierarchy are not felt to be needed. Rather, consumer-value people have a sense that the people who care most about participation in a program are the ones who should assume authority over decision making. In this value system one finds also that participants prefer to make the planning team and the planning time line as abbreviated and nonredundant as possible to move to action more quickly. In large congregations this approach means adding more full- and part-time program staff to move from idea to implementation with fewer committee volunteers and less time. In all sizes of congregations it means using more task forces and teams that represent a short-term commitment and a lesser need to check approvals.

Congregations are shifting their internal shapes to accommodate this turn in cultural values. Even the largest congregations are downsizing their governing boards. Several years ago I worked with a congregation of 2,000 members with a governing board of six leaders. Such congregations learned that where attention was once given to representation, so that all voices in the congregation would be present at meetings of the board, now attention needs to be given to communication and trust. Boards need to find and practice ways of listening to the multiple voices in the congregation that are not all represented on the board and don't care to be. Nonetheless, those voices need to be heard and need to have a clear feeling that they have been heard. Boards need also to find ways to tell people continually what they are doing and why they are doing it, so that trust can develop in an open environment in which there is no sense that conversations and decisions are hidden.

Both those who hold the GI value preferences and those who hold the consumer value preferences are concerned about good leadership. Despite this agreement, people of the two value systems can easily offend the others. A common concern voiced by clergy and key lay leaders is how to provide for all of the programs and services that the congregation wants if members won't join committees and help make it happen. At the same time, proponents of the consumer value system are offended by being asked to give time to a committee that has not been given authority to act, and being expected to sit through redundant meetings of planning and checking. They are often particularly offended when they must seek approvals from boards or people who are not interested in participating in the project being planned.

Leadership Observations of the Bimodal Congregation

The issues and experiences of the multigenerational congregation go far beyond the few examples outlined in this chapter. Generational value differences are also directly encountered in worship and education. Each congregation will undoubtedly find other places where it bumps into these value-system differences. Since the generational value-system differences are markers in a culturewide shift in values, congregations can expect to encounter these differences in any number of expressions. In fact, given the appropriate environment for learning and reflection, such as a leadership retreat setting, and given a time apart from decision making and problem solving, one can find it instructional and fun to invite leaders to explore where their congregation has encountered these generational value systems over the past few years.

In a later chapter we will discuss what leaders need to do to guide a multigenerational congregation effectively. New skills and assumptions are needed by leaders of bimodal congregations. These skills and assumptions were not needed in an earlier time when only the GI value system prevailed. The norms of that value system built a consensus within the congregation that provided a much easier path for leaders. But while we are describing what it is like to live in a multigenerational congregation, let's make at least three preliminary observations for leaders.

First, the differences between long-tenured and short-tenured members are natural. As part of a cultural shift, the bumps encountered in the congregation are part of a much larger, and essentially healthy, cultural picture of generational change. Some, of course, will mourn the loss of generational values that have meant the most to them and served

them well. But even here, a cyclical interpretation of human history suggests that we will, within several more generational cohorts, revisit and
reclaim some of the values that have currently fallen out of favor.

If we are able to see, and to help others to see, that these differences
in the congregation are natural, then they need not be approached as problems to be solved. Indeed, as I will point out later, these differences are
difficult to solve or to compromise in ways that satisfy all parties. More
important is the realization that if these differences are natural, we can
begin to see that the people representing conflicting value systems are not
necessarily ill-behaved, malicious people simply because they disagree with
what others are trying to do.

Too easily congregational leaders *begin* their assessment of "difficult"
members (that is, those who disagree with what the leaders are trying to
do) from a "pathological" point of view. They "diagnose" what is wrong
with the disagreeable other. Indeed, pathological people are present in some
congregations. However, I suspect that far fewer of these pathological folk
are present than the number leaders tend to point to. In a time in which most
clergy and many lay leaders have a basic level of training or familiarity with
psychology, it is too easy and convenient to dismiss a disagreeable other
with a pathological description suggesting that something is "wrong" with
someone who does not see things our own way. Beginning with the ac-
knowledgment that basic value differences will naturally be encountered in
healthy congregations allows leaders to put aside quick diagnoses of pathology. Leaders are then able to see that they are witnessing people who
are giving voice to different values and life lessons. If leaders help people
with value differences to engage each other responsibly, the conflict does
not threaten the congregation. To the contrary, a responsible engagement of
these differences helps to shape the faith tradition, and the congregation
will be able to live and speak more appropriately to a changing world.

Second, these differences may be natural, but they are also *difficult* to
live with. When one party wants to save the reserved funds as an act of
faithful stewardship, and one party wants to spend the reserved funds for
the same reason, it is difficult to find a satisfying compromise. One cannot
save the same dollars one is spending. To save and protect one portion and
to spend another portion of the asset may be a workable agreement that
both parties will allow. But the solution leaves each side feeling compromised in its sense of stewardship. Similarly, one cannot hope to fill all volunteer slots in the committee structure and simultaneously set whole groups of

people free to work on task forces or project teams—that is, one cannot without running out of volunteers and confusing committees and teams over issues of implementation and authority.

Because of the oppositional nature of the value differences, finding a satisfying compromise or a middle ground tends to be difficult. As I was working with one congregation, the leaders and I were able to describe the generational value-system preferences that were at the heart of their discomfort with applause in worship. People identified with the GI value system approached their worship time and space with the value of a spirituality of place; they were offended by the lack of formality and the nature of applause, which to them seemed more suitable to a secular performance. Those shaped by the consumer-value system approached the worship time and space as a stop on their spiritual journey, not unlike others; they did not consider it to have such clear sacred/secular boundaries. The worship space could be experienced as another venue for their active search and participation. With such assumptions, applause could quite naturally fit into a worship service. The group was able to see little room for compromise. To applaud would offend those of one value system. To prohibit applause would offend the others. I observed with this group that perhaps the only real compromise would be to allow people to clap with one hand! Fortunately, they laughed, and we were able to talk more deeply about what was important in worship for them together in the future.

Third, if these differences in the congregation are natural, and if they are difficult to address in ways that produce effective and satisfying compromises or solutions, then leaders need new assumptions and skills to work with the multigenerational congregation. These tools and strategies are needed for leaders who are clearly stuck between factions in the congregation. However, before moving on to describe these assumptions and skills, it is important for leaders to understand more about the unique dynamics of bimodal congregations, the subject of chapter 8.

CHAPTER 7

Biblical Glimpses: Part III

Not every congregation finds its biblical story easily. The tensions between generational cohorts or value-system factions can exacerbate feelings, making it difficult for members to find and maintain a balanced perspective. Among the values and practical skills that key leaders can bring to an anxious congregation are poise and balance. These qualities are essential to making the spiritual connection between the congregation's daily reality and its greater purpose.

In a small, historic congregation on the East Coast a battle broke out over the recently called new pastor. The local community had an old New England atmosphere, but it was expanding as new residents moved in. The wish to grow was clearly stated in the terms of call, and the pastor readily acknowledged that her role was to lead this congregation in welcoming and receiving new members. By her second year with the congregation, her efforts at welcoming were clearly paying off as increasing numbers of new people participated in the church. Overall the public acceptance of the newcomers was warm and open. But privately the long-tenured members shared phone calls and parking-lot discussions about changes that seemed to be getting out of hand.

The pastor bore the brunt of the criticism. Times of both formal and informal evaluation became awkward. She was criticized for spending too much time with new members and not showing up regularly for the church's Wednesday morning sewing group of older women. Rumors spread that she didn't spend much time at the hospital with several elderly inactive members, but that she drove one of the new members to the hospital emergency room and stayed with her all day. Some members voiced concern that she didn't initiate pastoral visits to the two long-tenured families who were most upset when the location of the annual summer picnic was changed.

When she was finally persuaded by one of the long-tenured members to visit the two distressed families, she surprised quite a few established leaders by not changing her mind and returning to the old picnic location. When she altered the music style of the early worship service and included folklike guitar singing led by several young and newly arrived families in the church—against the wishes of the 75-year-old organist, who had provided unpaid musical leadership for more than 25 years—many members concluded that this time, the pastor's action was the last straw.

The leaders had already held a congregational meeting at which a vote was taken on whether the pastor should be retained or asked to leave. The voting participants were split 50-50. The congregation was severely divided as I began to work with them. Long-tenured members recited prepared lists of what the pastor had done wrong; they pointed to numerous ways in which, under her leadership, they were losing their valued congregation. Newer, short-tenured members responded with stories of how the pastor's warmth and caring had led them to this congregation and how she had helped them get established in the church or assisted with family or personal dilemmas. The debate among members became pointed and personal in regard to the pastor's character and performance.

I needed to devise some measure of how this pastor was handling the criticism. In our interview I asked her how she was doing and what she was doing for self-care during this turbulent time. She acknowledged that she was having difficulties and that she often felt attacked. However, she added in a poised manner that she continually reminded herself that the criticisms were not all about her. She admitted that she had been a bit abrupt in making changes and that it may have been unwise to neglect visiting with established groups like the Wednesday sewing group. "But as much as they talk about me," she said, "this is really about the gospel." She had found the congregation's story.

She talked about Jesus' parable of the laborers in the vineyard (Matt. 20:1-16). In that story a landowner in need of laborers hires several men early in the morning, promising to pay them the usual daily wage, and sends them out into the vineyard to work. Needing more workers, he goes out again at nine in the morning, at noon, at three o'clock, and again at five in the afternoon—each time hiring more men. At evening, when the day's work is done, the laborers gather to be paid, and the landowner gives them all the same daily wage, no matter how long they have worked in the vineyard. The men who have worked all day are upset and "[grumble] against the landowner, saying, 'These last worked only one hour, and you have made them equal to us who have borne the burden of the day and the scorching heat.'" The landowner simply points out that he has fulfilled his promise by giving those who worked the longest the full day's wage. If he chooses to be generous to others who came later in the day, that is his privilege. The landowner ends by pointing out that "the last will be first, and the first will be last" in the kingdom of heaven.

The pastor said that the issue illuminated by this parable was really what her congregation was wrestling with. They had asked her to lead them in growth, and she had worked hard to invite and include new people. But the long-tenured members of the congregation, she said, began to be upset with the attention given to the newcomers. She pointed out that attention was the "wage" they were disputing. They carefully watched who received the "wages" or rewards of the pastor's attention, seats on the governing board and some committees, and the right to help make decisions. Some of the long-tenured members were still living on small farms that had been passed down through five generations. These people of the original families who settled the area and helped to create the town were not happy to see new people arrive and move into developments of homes being built on old farmland. They were not about to let these new members "take over" their church. The real wrestling, said the pastor, was going on inside the longtime members, who resented seeing the last people to arrive get first attention, while they, the members of the first families, could only surmise that their own opinions came last.

Yes, the debate centered on the pastor and her performance, but the real issue was the matter of being a spiritual community. Some of the less conflicted members were able to hear this biblical story and understand that it described their own experience. For these members the biblical story gave meaning and purpose to the larger conversation that others were having about the behavior of the pastor. As in this congregation, many of our uncomfortable multigenerational conversations have meaning beyond people's immediate concerns. Our congregations are truly wrestling with what it means to be spiritual communities.

The hard work of finding the spiritual connection for the congregation does not guarantee a smooth path or a successful ending. This church was so deeply divided that the pastor and leaders finally came to a shared conclusion that she would leave because her leadership had been so compromised by the conflict. While some members could not or would not listen to the biblical story that their pastor had found for them, others did—long-tenured and short-tenured alike. Members of the congregation were learning about their bimodal differences and their need to change. This congregation, however, had suffered some damage in its encounter with these differences.

CHAPTER 8

"In a Mirror Dimly": Dynamics of Bimodal Congregations

The much-quoted chapter on love in Paul's first letter to the Corinthians makes reference to a mirror: "For now we see in a mirror, dimly, but then we will see face to face" (1 Cor. 13:12). One expects a bit more from a mirror. Commonly we anticipate seeing an accurate, if reversed, reflection of ourselves when we look into a mirror, trusting the image to be true at a high level of detail. But not all mirrors are like that. The textual reference in the Oxford Annotated Bible to Paul's writing notes that the mirror of that era was "a polished metal surface not yielding a clear image."[1] In such a mirror the reflection is more suggestive than accurate. One sees shapes and images without much detail.

The somewhat distorted reflection of the polished metal mirror is like the way we and our leaders see the bimodal congregation. The shape is there, the pattern seems to fit, we're able to say "yes, that's us," but we are still puzzled by the detail that appears out of place.

To this point, my description of the bimodal congregation has been relatively simple. I have acknowledged the intentional stereotyping of the subgroups in a congregation. My argument is that the more simplified description of generational and tenure differences allows us to view the dominant value-system framework that rests beneath many of them. But once described, this basic picture seems distorted by individuals who don't follow the pattern and by behaviors that seem out of place or out of character for the individual, given his or her position in the congregation.

For example, I consulted with an East Coast Presbyterian church during a vitriolic dispute over its new senior pastor, a man in his late 30s who had a young family. He had been called to this congregation about two years before I was asked to consult with the leadership. He had succeeded the beloved founding pastor, who retired after a 23-year tenure.

Many members were registering their strong opinions that the young pastor just "isn't doing it right." They had multiple examples that they willingly shared in small listening groups that I conducted to gather data. This was clearly a bimodal congregation with substantial recent growth and two value systems at work. As one would guess, many of the complaints (well organized through petitions, anonymous letters, and intentional recruitment to get "our side" represented in the consultant's listening process) came from the older, longer-tenured members who adhered most closely to the GI value system. The behaviors and the tension all fit the pattern.

However, in one of the small listening groups, I realized that I was hearing a number of younger members who, oddly enough, were carrying the older members' messages. They offered examples of ways that the new minister was not "doing it right," and argued that he should, therefore, be forced out. One young woman in her early 30s was particularly emphatic about the pastor's misstatements and misdeeds. She then described how disappointed she was for her church *now that she had moved across town and was active as a leader in another congregation!* Clearly something did not fit here. Despite her youth, her behavior better reflected the GI value system of identity through membership—with expectations that the new pastor conform to the practices of the group. Like other GI value holders, even though she now participated in another congregation and did not attend this one, she remained a formal member who expected that she had the right and the authority to insist that the new pastor conform—even when she wasn't present!

If the bimodal dynamic of coexisting value systems in the congregation reflects reality, it is, indeed, a dim mirror that must allow for distortions such as the foregoing example. These distortions of the multigenerational congregation are supported by a few dynamics that are worth noting. I will explore three of them.

Membership Tenure and Individual Age

Part of the confusion in trying to understand the bimodal congregation is the relationship between membership tenure and the age of the individual. The basic measure offered for the bimodal congregation is tenure—how long people have been members or participants. Using that measure, we can uncover the basic pattern of the bimodal congregation with a large grouping of long-tenured members, a large grouping of short-tenured members, and a dearth of bridge people in between. But then, curiously, the conversation shifts away from membership tenure to the value systems of generational cohorts—an issue of age, not tenure. What is the relationship between tenure of membership and the age of the individual as we describe these bimodal, multigenerational congregations?

A primary lesson of working with bimodal congregations is the high correlation between age and tenure of membership. But tenure—the length of one's membership or participation—is the more dominant factor that will determine a member's behavior in that congregation.

It stands to reason that, though there are exceptions, the longer-tenured members tend to be older, and shorter-tenured members tend to be younger. For this reason these two subgroups tend to hold different cultural value systems that are most easily identified with age cohorts. A critical mass of people of similar age cohorts in each of these two larger subsystems will carry the dominant value system of their cohort and imprint that value system on the congregation. Therefore, the longer-tenured portion of the congregation is basically aligned with the GI value system, even though members of that group can fully understand and, at times, appreciate consumer values. Similarly, the shorter-tenured portion of the congregation is basically aligned with the consumer value system, even though participants in that group can understand and, at times, appreciate GI values.

The confusing fact is that age and tenure, while highly correlated for most people in a congregation, do not correlate for all individuals. When this is the case, it seems that *tenure* is the more dominant value. For example, a 30-year-old member may clearly live on the consumer-value side of the cultural watershed in daily life. However, if he has been an active member of a congregation for, say, 20 years or more, he will behave in accordance with the GI value system *within the congregation*. While he may fully participate in consumer values in daily life, in the congregation he will more likely behave according to the GI values. (This was clearly the case with the young woman in the example on page 102.)

Similarly, it is not unusual for a new member to join a congregation in her mid- to late 60s or 70s. Such a person is clearly steeped in the cultural value system of the GIs, and she will understand and support that part of congregational life rather easily. Nonetheless, this older woman will have joined this congregation with a real sensitivity to consumer values. Like her younger counterparts, she will have "shopped" a number of congregations, probably of different denominations, before finding this one that best meets her needs and preferences—a primary consumer orientation. Like their younger consumer-value counterparts, new members over 60 will remain active participants in the congregation if their needs and preferences are met from the start. But like their younger counterparts, they will leave silently to continue shopping if their needs are disappointed before a sense of identity and membership develops.

For example, a retired couple in their late 60s joined a congregation in the recreational mountain area of eastern Pennsylvania, their new retirement home. As new members, they discovered that the congregation was in the throes of a dispute: Members who appreciated the new contemporary service, offered as an alternative second worship setting, were in conflict with those who disliked the informality of the new setting. The traditionalists were indignant that the time of their service had been changed to accommodate the contemporary service. The alternative service was more like the worship that this couple had enjoyed in their previous congregation back in New Jersey, and it was a part of what attracted them to this church. As they participated in a small listening group—part of the consultation I was leading in this congregation—this retired couple offered two fundamental messages. The first was that they understood why the new contemporary service might be upsetting to other long-tenured members who were used to the traditional worship. The second message, however, was that if the other members forced this pastor to leave and brought the contemporary worship to an end, they would certainly leave as well. While they were in their 60s and understood the GI posture, their position was more recognizable as consistent with the consumer-value system.

It would seem, then, that age and tenure tend to be correlated in congregations. But when some individuals or groups do not fit that pattern, the tenure of membership or participation is the more dominant variable, the one that determines the behavior and positions they assume *in the congregation.* This dominance of tenure is based on the function of group norms and the power that "norming" exerts on individual behavior.

According to Susan Wheelan, professor of organizational dynamics at Temple University, Philadelphia:

> "[N]orms represent collective value judgments about how members should behave and what should be done in the group. Norms are necessary if the group is to coordinate its efforts and accomplish its goals. Without behavioral predictability, chaos reigns.

For example, it would be dangerous to drive a car if we were uncertain whether others would obey traffic signals. Since we can predict that most citizens will obey them, we feel safe when driving. In like manner, a group has a task. That task requires members to behave in certain ways in order to succeed. If members' behaviors were unpredictable or chaotic, there would be little hope of task accomplishment. Thus, norms are established.[2]

Norms are the informal rules of groups. Not codified in formal documents, often not easily described by the very people who practice them, organizational norms are nonetheless agreements on how people should behave as a part of the group. These rules are passed on to others by example and by the imposition of sanctions in a process of "norming." In other words, those who understand the norms behave in accordance with these informal rules and demonstrate "appropriate" behavior. As new people join the group, those who quickly conform to the established group norms are rewarded with inclusion and approval. Those who do not learn quickly and do not accommodate the norms find themselves sanctioned by disapproving comments, looks, or signals (such as exclusion from conversations), indicating that they are not well received. The process of norming is a powerful dynamic in group life that builds common identity and cohesion. Norming provides a shared understanding of how things work in the group. This building of shared norms allows the group a common life. Group members can take action toward their goals or tasks without having to stop at every step along the way to decide how to act.

In the example on page 102, the woman in her 30s who behaved in accord with the GI values of group identity was simply conforming to the norms of conflict she learned in her long association with this church in which she grew up. She was free to participate in another congregation on the other side of town that met the consumer needs of her young family. But as a still-formal member of the church of her childhood, when she returned in the role of faithful member, she easily reverted to, and was expected to conform to, the norms she learned there.

Norms do not control all aspects of the individual's behavior. In observing congregations or the behaviors of individuals in subgroups within congregations, one does not commonly find people moving lockstep in identical behavior. Even with dominant value systems that exercise enormous power over individuals, one does not expect that all people in a generational cohort will offer identical arguments or exhibit identical behaviors. Although norms provide both direction and boundaries for behavior, ample room is left for individuality. As Susan Wheelan explains:

> It is important to keep in mind that groups do not create norms for all behaviors, attitudes, or feelings. Norms are created to ensure conformity with essential and important group values and beliefs. Consequently, while the impact of groups on individuals is very significant, this influence is felt only in relation to certain core values and beliefs. In other areas, the individual has some latitude to express his or her uniqueness. As a result, individual differences will be noted even within groups composed of persons with similar socio-identity profiles.[3]

The challenge for the leader is to observe the dynamics within the bimodal congregation but to lay aside any expectation that all experiences and behaviors will conform to a prescribed and predictable model. Rather, the leader should be able to identify and help others to see the basic themes and patterns of tenured behavior normed by generational values. These basic themes and patterns of tenured behavior in the congregation are the truer expressions of the values held and the commitments made by this body of people.

We All Want It Our Way

The second dynamic related to the dim mirror in which we view the bimodal congregation is the cultural reality that we all want our own way. A congregational norming process demonstrates behavior consistent with chosen values and censures behaviors inconsistent with those values. A cultural norming process also operates in people's lives beyond the realm of congregational participation. We are a product not only of the groups (such as church or synagogue) that we join, but also of the culture in which we live.

The easier of the assumptions from our discussion so far is that the GI generational cohort simply conforms to group expectations and is content to accept whatever the group wants. The corollary assumption for the consumer value cohort is that these individuals all want to have life on their own terms. The reality, however, is that we encounter people of all ages and generational cohorts in our congregations who "want it my way." This cultural phenomenon goes beyond our congregations and requires a deeper understanding of changing cultural value systems.

At a watershed moment, when two dominant value systems are living side by side in tension, we find that even those living most deeply within one value system at least recognize and at times appreciate the other value system. The differences between the GI and consumer-value systems are dramatic. Yet it is common for people on both sides of the generational divide to live with a clear sensitivity to the watershed—to have at least an awareness of the differences represented in the value system of the other. Those born and nurtured in one value system can still understand and respond to the markers of the other value system.

For example, the baby boomers and successive consumer-value cohorts were shaped by the values of instant gratification. The sexual revolution encouraged people not to wait for marriage before becoming sexually active. The drug culture prompted people to alter their moods chemically without waiting for a better day to come. The civil rights movement redefined the fundamental relationship between blacks and whites without waiting for the slow process of legislation to lead the way. Undergirded by an economy that made more resources available to more people and a marketing and advertising industry that constantly urged people to buy before they had the cash in hand, the possibility of instant gratification became a dominant shaper of the new value system.

At the time of such a dramatic shift, the people closest to the watershed divide separating GI values from consumer values can participate in the new cultural lessons of immediacy while also understanding and responding to the lessons of deferred pleasure that are being left behind. In his cultural analysis of the legacy of the 1960s, Myron Magnet (editor of the *City Journal*, the quarterly published by the conservative think tank Manhattan Institute) points out that for all their insistence on immediacy and liberation movements, when it came to their professions and life work, the baby boomers never lost their essential work ethic of deferred pleasure.[4] Within the congregation this factor contributes to the confusion of understanding individual behavior. Consumer-oriented people are sensitive to elements that are aligned (or not aligned) with their immediate needs in the congregation, but they are simultaneously exercising self-discipline for the long haul in their careers to achieve goals that require sacrifices of deferred pleasure. In other words, they follow some norms within the congregation, but they also respond to a set of cultural norms that better serves another part of their lives.

Similar observations can be made of members of the GI cohort. Steeped in group conformity and deferred pleasure, they may rail against the "self-centeredness" of the consumer generations, but they have also experienced the rise of sophistication in the advertising and marketing industries. They too participate freely in immediate gratification through credit purchasing plans and responses to targeted marketing. And they like it. These people form a major segment of the market for TV merchandising channels such as QVC, which depends upon the consumer's penchant for impulse buying from the comfort of home. GI generation people enjoy browsing mail-order catalogues as much as any other generational segment. These are the people who, on weekday mornings in multiple mid-Atlantic states, fill the buses headed for Atlantic City. A fairly modest bus fare gets the rider a day trip to the ocean with $10 worth of quarters and delivers passengers to the very door of the promise of immediate gratification.

These tendencies too contribute to the confusion of trying to under-stand congregations where GI-value-oriented folk insist on disciplines and practices of group conformity in the congregation, but then practice con-sumer values and behaviors in other parts of their lives. This inconsistency often leads to frustration in congregations when these people insist that all committees be filled with volunteers, or that previous programs be repeated. In doing so, they are working out of the norms of GI behavior that rest on group practices and sacrificial commitment. Yet simultaneously these mem-bers may be announcing that they themselves cannot help with the commit-tee work or program planning because they have planned a retirement trip or have already "done their time." In so doing they are responding to the consumer values of individualism and instant gratification while laying the expectation of deferred pleasure on others.

If there is a shared viewpoint for many of the subgroups or shadings along the continuum of shifting value systems, it is the belief that each group should "have it our own way." Because people of both value systems most closely aligned with the cultural watershed have experienced the transition to immediate gratification, it seems that those on both sides of the divide have learned that their own preference should win the day. While Burger King must surely be fighting for its own market share in the highly competi-tive fast-food business, it won one cultural skirmish long ago by announcing that you and everyone else should "have it your way." While dominant value systems remain in conflict within our congregations, and while even those most deeply entrenched in one system can exhibit contradictory individual behavior, nonetheless the one conviction most easily held in common is the expectation that, as an individual, "I am right for me," and "I should have it the way I want it." In a day when the mirror reflecting our communities of faith allows us to see general patterns, but not details, what is most clear is how difficult it is to build healthy community in the midst of these differences.

Generations Do Not Speak Well of Each Other

Some anthologists report that Mark Twain said, "[W]hen I was a boy of fourteen, my father was so ignorant I could hardly stand to have the old man around. But when I got to be twenty-one, I was astonished at how much he had learned in seven years."[5] Twain described well the judgmental attitude that all generations assume in encounters with other generations. The fallacy in Twain's quip is that generations tend not to progress in seven years, or 70, to a fuller appreciation of other generations. For the most part, generations do not speak well of each other. This third dynamic contributes additional confusion in congregations. The judgmental and defensive positions that generational cohorts all too quickly assume when they encounter differences will shift the agenda immediately from learning about and negotiating differences to the task of assigning blame—which becomes a contest between "right and wrong."

In their book *Generations Apart: Xers vs. Boomers vs. the Elderly*, Richard Thau, executive director of Third Millennium, a nonpartisan advocacy group for Americans born after 1960, and Jay Heflin, a free-lance writer, have compiled a testament to the discomfort that generations feel with one another. In an introduction the editors describe the set of essays as a "sampling of writings from members of one generation taking exception to the opinions of other generations."[6] To demonstrate the historic continuity of this principle of discomfort and argument between generations, Thau and Heflin offer sample essays published in the *Atlantic Monthly* in 1911.[7] Apart from the more formal language of an earlier time, these early essays could easily be mistaken for present-day generational evaluations.

Part of the experience of a generational cohort is to grow up with a set of life lessons that belong uniquely to a group of people born at a particular historic moment with its own cauldron of problems, pressures, and opportunities. The common location in history experienced by each new generation is understood to some extent as the "product" of the labors of the previous generation's labors. Like all good adolescents, each generational cohort grows up differentiating itself from the parent generation by focusing on the parents' weaknesses or overused strengths that define the fatal flaw that the older generation carried. Generations, like children in a family, find their place in the sun by identifying and standing against the limitations seen in the ones that went before.

The GI generation was shaped by its markers to be a heroic people who could organize to take on economic disaster, environmental challenges, and a global war; and to turn the world around. As GIs returned home after the war, they industriously created an amazingly productive economy, safe and stable housing, an educational boom, and a sense of community order and organization. Community order reached so deeply that informal sandlot baseball was transformed into a massive organization called Little League.

As recipients of this newly structured world, succeeding generational cohorts reaped the benefits of the GI generation. But then to define its own identity, the next generation focused on the lack of freedom, the limits placed on feelings, and the absence of spirit that could accompany excessive structure and organization. The baby boomers stood against their predecessor cohort with this judgment: the boomers needed liberation from the sterility of the generation that went before. This new generation and its cohorts pursued liberation and license in search of the spirit that was absent from their seniors. In opposition to their predecessors, the agents of freedom created a brave new world that searched for meaning, offered equality and justice more freely, and honored the individual, who had previously been understood only as a part of the group.

Those who followed after—the busters, Xers, and millennials—benefited in turn from their inheritance. But they also had their chances to stand against the fatal flaws of their predecessors, asserting that the freedom championed by the boomers became license, that justice spilled over into political correctness, and that the liberation that produced so many divorces should be tempered with caution and responsibility. Like previous cohorts, they took their turn in correcting the excesses or repairing the flaws produced by the overused strengths and overpracticed lessons of the previous cohorts. As in all healthy systems, successive generations offered corrections as a system began to tilt out of balance. But the process of healthy generational balancing rests on resistance that comes from an evaluation of the generation that went before. This process supports the ongoing tendency of each generation to evaluate and speak ill of other generations.

As Strauss and Howe note, "[O]ne lesson of the cycle is that every generational type has its own special vision of the American Dream."[8] Strauss and Howe note, quoting the work of sociologist and scholar Giuseppe Ferrari, that the generational resistance to surrounding generations forms a repeating cycle:

> [A] revolutionary generation launches a new idea, a reactionary generation battles against that idea, a humanizing generation uses that idea to establish community and build political institutions, and a preparatory generation subtly undermines that harmony, after which the cycle repeats.[9]

The result is that successive generations historically do not speak well of each other. Tom Brokaw's best-selling book *The Greatest Generation* told the historic story of the GI generation.[10] But it is instructive to read his account not just for the story of a war-centered generation but also for the subtext of generational evaluation and judgment that permeates the telling. The stories of this one high-profile generation include copious notations about their disappointments with the generations to follow:

> A common lament of the World War II generations is the absence today of personal responsibility (p. 24).

> The idea of personal responsibility is such a defining characteristic of the World War II generation that when the rules changed later, these men and women were appalled (p. 39).

> Peggy says young couples these days "don't fight long enough. It's too easy to get a divorce. We've had our arguments, but we don't give up. When my friends ask whether I ever consider divorce I remind them of the old saying, 'We've thought of killing each other, but divorce? Never'" (p. 239).

It takes effort and thoughtfulness not to be caught up in generational evaluations. One of the healthiest and most insightful presentations I have heard on cross-generational analysis came from Tom Freston, chairman and CEO of MTV, the very young organization that provides TV entertainment to GenXers. Speaking at a National Press Club luncheon, he offered an interpretation of the GenX generational cohort, based on MTV's market research.[11] At point after point, Freston was able to redraw members of this generational cohort as family-oriented (when they were frowned upon for never leaving home), as cross-cultural (when white kids were criticized for strutting around in baggy pants and baseball caps worn backward, while inner-city black kids were wearing Tommy Hilfiger), as tolerant and inclusive (when they were rebuked for their fascination with Asian, African, and Middle Eastern pop stars of whom their parents had never heard). Using the same data and behaviors cited by their generational critics, Freston offered positive definitions and perspectives on this "generation of slackers." Generational cohorts do not speak well of each other and often need help to see what is positive in the differences that irritate predecessors and successors alike.

The judgmental lenses used by successive generational cohorts to look critically at other cohorts confuse our understanding of the bimodal congregation. Normal generational behavior is weighted with positive and negative valences, depending upon one's generational point of view. Little neutral territory stands between competing value systems as a place for leaders to negotiate clear decisions and to seek agreement.

The basic dynamics noted in this chapter—tenure vs. age, all wanting it their own way, and generational cohorts not speaking well of each other—make differences even more difficult to identify and negotiate, thus increasing the challenges that leaders face. Long-tenured members of all ages and generational cohorts who conform to the established norms in congregations will continue to confuse and "disprove" any generational descriptions used by congregational leaders to help people talk about their differences descriptively. The desire of all members to have it their own way—an experience shared across all contemporary generational cohorts—heightens the tension by moving people more quickly toward win-lose solutions. The propensity of all generational cohorts to speak badly of other cohorts invites people to understand their differences as problems to be solved rather than as opportunities to learn and to practice spiritual community.

"For now we see in a mirror, dimly." The task of leadership in a bimodal congregation is clouded by the internal dynamics of this congregation. It would certainly be easier for leaders and members alike if all individuals of similar age and shared generational cohort behaved uniformly and with understanding of other cohorts. Life, however, is not ordered that way. Creativity and change are not so predictable. Leaders need to master the basic description of generational and value differences that drive the individuals in the congregation. Leaders must also allow for the messiness of real life, in which the basic patterns will be stretched and influenced by the dynamics identified in this chapter. Far from adopting a conclusion that the congregation is out of control or that individual members are behaving inappropriately, the more helpful posture of faith suggests that God is doing something new in the congregation. Creation is always messy. Paying attention to the larger patterns of cultural value change, while allowing individual deviations from that pattern, enables leaders to support and participate in the new creation that God has begun in our midst.

CHAPTER 9

"What's a Leader to Do?" Leadership in the Middle

You are sitting with the finance committee, whose agenda is to make a recommendation to the governing board on the use of interest and dividends from the restricted funds that support your congregation's work. The investments, having grown consistently over the past several years, now produce a substantial annual income. At the same time, it has become increasingly difficult to support the growing annual operations budget from member giving. This long-running conversation about the use of investment income has continued for several months; now the committee is deadlocked. Half of the group firmly insists that all interest and dividends must be reinvested to provide security for the future in an uncertain investment climate. The other half contends that reinvestment is an irresponsible way to "feather our own nest" and that at least a portion of the income should be made available to expand and improve the program life of the congregation.

If you are a leader in a multigenerational, bimodal congregation, current experience teaches that you have no easy task. At its best it might be compared to a Laurel and Hardy comedy routine in which the pair try to do two opposite things at the same time. As they flip back and forth, each new action undoes the one before, to the delight of the audience. Working with people to save and spend the same money—or both to encourage and to prohibit applause in worship—can fit this Laurel and Hardy routine easily enough. The standard comedic response is to work harder and faster to solve the problem. The result is a situation that falls apart very quickly.

If, at its best, leading a bimodal congregation feels like a Laurel and Hardy festival, at its worst can feel like a deadly trap. Sitting with a deadlocked finance committee for a third monthly session of impasse can lead to a common response of frustrated committee members—blaming the leader. At the point of evaluation, frustrated members in bimodal congregations often blame the leader for failing to provide clear and unifying direction. With the natural opposites that underlie the generational differences in the congregation, leaders regularly find themselves in the unresolved double bind defined by Gregory Bateson in chapter 1.

The leader lives and works in the middle. As noted earlier, whatever the tenure of key leaders—long-tenured or recently arrived—the leader lives in the middle between the two dominant value systems. When the bimodal clusters of members become uncomfortable or frustrated with their differences, they look to the "bridge people" in the middle. Not surprisingly, bimodal congregations frequently argue about the adequacy and effectiveness of their leaders.

It is also no surprise that leaders in bimodal congregations commonly report feeling overworked and underappreciated. Beneath the surface agreement that appears to unite the congregation, little or no consensus obtains on what is important and how the congregation should move ahead. Clergy regularly report on the surprising but necessary investment of time and energy in "shuttle diplomacy," in which leaders must travel back and forth between disputing subgroups to interpret one group's position to the other. In an earlier day, when the congregation was uniformly guided by the GI generation's value system, leaders could depend on a broadly shared consensus. A congregation with a commonly held identity and sense of mission, even if unarticulated, evaluated leadership primarily by the easier criterion of managing the agreement that already existed in the congregation.

The current bimodal congregation is quite a different beast. Marvelously countercultural in a time of developing consumer pure-market segments, congregations continue to be an exception to the rule. While the larger culture continuously invites us to segment ourselves into smaller and smaller identity tribes of preferential similarities, congregations call us together across those differences to find a larger common spiritual identity with those not in our identity tribes or pure-market segments. As such, congregations continue to serve as major building blocks of social capital in our communities by providing a place of purposeful engagement where people gather across their differences. But an organizational price must be paid for this countercultural posture. The cost is borne most heavily by leaders who are responsible for developing consensus and shared identity among the culturally honored differences that people bring to the congregation. Old standards of evaluating leaders on the management of assumed unity no longer fit. The challenge of leadership has become more complex.

Old measures of widespread harmony are no longer easily achieved and no longer describe effective leadership.

What's a Leader to Do?

To acknowledge that leading a multigenerational, bimodal congregation is difficult is not to diminish the value and importance of such bimodal congregations to both our faith traditions and our communities. I hope that readers have discovered the underlying conviction in this book that bimodal congregations are healthy, normal, and unusually productive. The bimodal congregation is actively shaping and passing our traditions and disciplines of faith from one generation to another. The disputes encountered, the decisions made, the practices altered are all steps taken to prepare living faith traditions to address the people of the future.

Along with shaping faith, these congregations also build—and rebuild—community in a fragmented age. At a recent training event with denominational executives, a participant told of a pastor from her association who visited a member in the hospital. The pastor came across a young woman who had recently given birth to her first child. What struck the pastor was that this woman was crying deeply at a moment that others would assume to be joyful. Introducing herself, the pastor discovered that the woman was frightened and alone because she and her husband had moved far from their families. Her mother could not travel to be with her and to help with the baby. With a membership dominated by the GI generation, the pastor realized she had a congregation full of surrogate mothers for this young woman. Working quietly, the pastor began connecting GI-era mothers to young women with children who lived far from their own mothers. Crossing generational boundaries, mixing pure markets, and blending identity tribes, this congregation was adding social capital to its greater community in ways that have disappeared from most other organizations and institutions.

The work and worth of these bimodal congregations are made possible as leaders help their members encounter, understand, and manage their differences and difficulties. The value of the work is not helped by leaders who smooth over the differences, try to keep disputing parties apart, or work double-time trying to keep everyone happy by being all things to all people. The goal of keeping everyone happy in a bimodal congregation diminishes the work of the congregation. As the leader or leaders assume the responsibility for finding solutions to people's discomfort, the real work of shaping the faith and congregational life for the next generations is slowed. Pretending that all members can shape congregational life in their preferred image does not help generations and cultural subgroups negotiate how to live together, share worship, or pass on the faith.

What then can leaders do? I will point to four principles or practices. These will not solve the problems of the bimodal congregation, diminish the differences, or make everyone more comfortable. They will, however, support the essential tasks of the generational work to be done in these congregations and share responsibility for the health of congregational life with the larger membership. These principles and practices are:

- Moving to the balcony,
- Working descriptively,
- Seeking common space, and
- Installing civility.

Leaders are discovering that whole new sets of skills are needed to address the watershed moment of giant cultural and technological shifts. However, as one works with bimodal congregations, these four principles and practices offer helpful leverage points to translate discomfort into community, and differences into ministry.

Moving to the Balcony

The place of daily life, work, and ministry is reactive space. No matter how we plan our day, we can expect our plans to be interrupted. When I ask groups how many people use daily "to do" lists, a substantial number of hands always go up. When I ask how many people have ever thrown out their lists by midmorning because of what awaited them when they arrived at work, a similar number of hands go up. This time, however, the gesture is accompanied by laughter and a recognition of our common plight.

Daily life is reactive space, not reflective space. We revert quickly to action modes in which we respond to immediate challenges by doing something. Our action modes are commonly guided by problem-solving frameworks in which we quickly assess "What's wrong here?" and "What do we need to do to make it right?" In fact, this problem-solving reflex serves us well—that is, when we are faced with a problem. The catch is that bimodal congregations are not necessarily problems. Although they seem problematic when differences surface and resist compromise, these multigenerational congregations are in fact healthy, productive arenas where people live out their faith and shape their traditions. Moving too quickly to "solve" the differences as problems can force the divergent voices of the congregation into a win-lose argument. People will move to defeat each other, and the work of faith development will be brought to a halt.

The alternative is for leaders to help people *learn* from one another. But the shift from *doing* something about our differences to *learning* about our differences requires a different space. Leaders need to move from reactive space of daily engagement to "balcony space," where reflection and learning are possible. Balcony space is a concept coined by Ronald Heifetz and David Laurie, teachers and writers connected with the Harvard Leadership Project.[1] Moving to the balcony allows one to look at the pattern, the big picture that can be lost in the details and pressures of daily life.

Professional football provides a helpful example. The action is on the field, where teams engage each other with problem-solving strategies and where each side tries to overpower the other. The coach is on the sideline with trainers and assistants, who are all busy. But where do they get their most helpful information? It comes from balcony space. The offensive and defensive coordinators are sitting several levels up in the stands with binoculars and a phone system. These are the people who watch the big picture. They see the whole field, while players and coach are too close to the action to see beyond the problem of the immediate moment. The balcony people are not nearly so active as the coach and players on the field. They sit and do the hard work of learning—of looking for patterns and trends, of checking statistics, of reviewing options, of dreaming up possibilities. Then they give their information, the product of their learning, to the coach on the field, where it can make a difference. The balcony work makes the action on the field purposeful and productive. Instead of always working reactively, learning from the balcony adds a strategic element to the game— pointing to where the players need to align and cooperate, drawing attention to opportunities to advance, identifying where team or individual efforts have been self-defeating.

In similar fashion, balcony space and learning can inform daily action in the congregation. Leaders need to step away from never-ending daily responsibilities and problem solving. They need to find some time in balcony space to glimpse the bigger picture and its connection to the congregation's purpose. The conflict for leaders is that balcony space is most needed at the very moment that differences are most painfully felt, and uncompromising pinches between generational value systems are pushing for answers—for action. Leaders of bimodal congregations need to manage their anxiety and move to the balcony instead of taking the heroic stand of coaching one team in the congregation to defeat the other.

Balcony learning best takes place in space where action and decisions are not expected. It is difficult to do good balcony work in the same room where the governing board meets or during board meeting time. Similarly, committee meetings or congregational meetings intended to resolve an issue are not good balcony learning times. The problem is that leaders try to make their decisions at an action time and in an action space. To engage people in an action space with a balcony learning agenda often produces negative results. Accustomed to being in an action mode at a board meeting, people will leave a balcony discussion in that space convinced that it was not a productive meeting because no decisions were made.

There are, of course, situations in which a leader can engage others in learning discussions only during board or committee meetings. Asking for additional time may seem an imposition on people already overwhelmed by their responsibilities. In such settings leaders need to negotiate for a portion of the board's time and agenda at regular meetings, but clearly inform people that they are being asked to learn and reflect, not "do." To make the balcony time productive, the leader must tell others that for the next 20 or 30 minutes they will not be asked to decide anything or solve any problem. They will be asked, instead, to learn something about all congregations; then they will be asked to talk about how the new learning helps them to understand their own congregation. The appropriate "action" to request in this setting is to invite people to spend time in the following days and weeks observing and reflecting on their congregation using the new information and insights, talking with one another about the insights, and using their new understanding in their prayers and discernments for their congregation.

If such limited times as segments of a board meeting are the only opportunities for learning and balcony work, the leader must design multiple smaller discussions. After the bimodal model is introduced in one discussion, the next meeting might explore the generational value differences over the use of reserved funds. Successive meetings might deal with differences over missions and worship. Finally, the leader will begin conversations about where "we in our own congregation" are experiencing our bimodal differences and will perhaps present a graph of the tenure of the congregation's own membership to explore how closely it parallels the pattern of bimodal congregations.

Obviously, these learning conversations are much richer and more productive—and more fun—when representatives of both of the cultural-watershed value systems are in the same room, and when they are encouraged to tell their own stories and speak from their own experience. Learning is more effective when we help people move from the theory and the general practice of all congregations to our own stories, experiences, and insights.

This balcony work is often most effective in separate settings in which the time and place differ from those of normal work and decision making. Leadership weekend retreats are prime times for learning. Weekday luncheon discussions can be used in some settings. A special leaders' forum for several weeks during regular adult learning times such as Sunday school or Bible study might be considered. A leader may choose to host several evenings of discernment or discussion at his or her home with the group seated around a fireplace or a coffeepot. Adults learn best when treated as adults and not as adolescent learners. Books are good learning tools because they often present balcony ideas. Providing copies of a book and inviting people to read offers a path into a deeper conversation in which participants share the same ideas and language. Descriptive videos are effective since they present the ideas quickly and invite people to respond to what the group viewed together.

The leader's responsibility is to introduce balcony work and to lead others into balcony space. It is not the leader's job to determine what others will learn from their balcony experience. The leader cannot control the conclusions of others and must, in fact, be willing to be a co-learner with the group. If willing to be a co-learner, the leader will more fully discover, sometimes with surprise or disappointment, what learnings the group is able to draw from its balcony time.

Working Descriptively

In situations where people are frustrated, angry, or dealing with difficult decisions, I tell the following story. It clarifies the difference between *description* and *evaluation* and suggests that these two modes of working, often confused, have very different consequences.

If I am driving my car at 55 miles per hour in a residential area where the posted speed limit is 35 mph and my wife, Lynne, is with me, she can choose to be either *descriptive* or *evaluative*. If she chooses to be descriptive, Lynne might say, "You are driving 55. This is a residential area posted at 35. I see children playing around here. I feel upset." These are descriptive statements. They carry accurate information about the situation. Lynne also describes her feelings. While she is not reporting all good and happy news to me, it is simply descriptive information. When someone gives you a description, you can negotiate. You can keep the conversation going and try to be creative. You can look for alternatives. I might say to Lynne, "You're right, I'd better slow down." I might say to her, "You're right, but we're late. Help me watch for kids!" And she might respond, "Pull over and let me drive." Whatever path we take, the conversation will continue because we are working with a description.

If, however, I am driving my car at 55 mph in a residential area where the posted speed limit is 35 mph and Lynne chooses to be evaluative, she might turn to me and say, "Gil, you are really a lousy driver"—clearly an evaluation. When someone gives you an evaluation, there is often no negotiation. Conversation ends abruptly. I am put in a position in which there is only one thing I can do. Quite simply, I must speed up!

When I ask people the difference between description and evaluation and why I must speed up, some in the group inevitably declare that it has something to do with gender differences or the inherent limitations of male driving behavior. Despite a possible grain of truth in such attempts at wit, the difference between the effect of description and the effect of evaluation is much more fundamental and universal. The way we receive and process information is at the heart of this functional difference. The difference lies at the very level at which our brains work.[2]

Evaluation is perceived as a threat. When threatening stimuli are perceived, the human brain manages this information in its most ancient portions, which are programmed for survival (the brain stem or "reptilian brain") or for the fight/flight reflex (the limbic system or "mammalian brain"). In the fight/flight reflex the perception of a threat leads to an autonomic response of moving either toward the threat (fight) or away from the threat (flight). In the fight mode we tend to attack. In my driving story, the fight response would prompt an attack from me on Lynne's driving ability or some other personal characteristic, and I would indeed speed up rather than heed her evaluation. No doubt an argument would ensue, and our need to be anywhere on time would be forgotten. In the flight mode we distance ourselves from the attack and assume a defensive posture. This time in the driving story I might defend my driving ability or perhaps just go quiet and sullen, not wanting to provoke an argument but also no longer effectively participating in the relationship.

Most important, both the reptilian and mammalian portion of the brain are automatic. There is no premeditative state or thoughtful work going on here. The responses to evaluation are reflexive and automatic, commonly pushing people into battle with one another or pushing them away from each other and straining the relationship.

Speech perceived as evaluation evokes a less-than-thoughtful response in the other. But when perceived and received as description, the information engages the neocortex of the brain—the largest portion of the brain, which manages thinking processes such as diagnosis, synthesis, and creativity. It is here that thoughtful work is done and learning occurs.

When leaders are dealing with generational differences in the congregation, they must work carefully to be descriptive, and they must model descriptive statements for others. Since generational cohorts commonly think and speak evaluatively about one another (see chapter 8), leaders must practice self-reflective behaviors to avoid evaluating rather than describing. Writing about the (Murray) Bowen therapeutic family-systems theory, psychiatrist Roberta Gilbert suggests that the language of leadership is accurate description:

It is not necessary to label and qualify all the different kinds of feelings that exist in human life. The diagnosis and description of subtle and even obvious differences can lead to a focus on pathology which then becomes an end in itself. Diagnosing pathology doesn't change anything. If one thinks, instead, in general terms of the emotional intensity or "anxiety" that exists in a system, time and energy are freed to think about options for managing it.[3]

Gilbert points out that it is not helpful for leaders to begin with diagnosis of what is pathological—wrong or limited about people or a situation. Such diagnoses are evaluations. Indeed, this automatic response is programmed into all of us. Leaders must do the hard work of moving beyond the quick evaluation to the deeper description that accurately reflects the experience of others in a way that can be understood and accepted.

Leaders must therefore be careful and deliberate in their use of words to develop a much richer descriptive vocabulary. The adjectives and adverbs chosen need to convey descriptions without attributing value or intent. The task is to describe accurately for others what is, without assigning goodness or badness to it, helpfulness or harm. The leadership position requires one to start from the assumption that a behavioral difference encountered in the congregation is a normal and natural expression of life lessons for the person or group. What needs to be accurately described, shared, and interpreted to others is the normative behavior that we all practice because of our generational life lessons, but that nevertheless baffles or offends others because these life lessons are different for other generational cohorts.

Leaders must serve as models in this search to understand normative behavior, because others in the congregation will not easily start from the perspective of accurate description. People more naturally start from a position of blaming. The much more common way for all of us to manage discomfort or offense that comes from experiencing differences is to begin with evaluation. But our next step is to move toward blame or an explanation that centers on what is wrong or limited about the person with whom we have experienced the discomfort. Psychologists call this tendency the Fundamental Attribution Error (FAE) which suggests that

[W]hen it comes to interpreting other people's behavior, human beings invariably make the mistake of overestimating the importance of fundamental character traits and underestimating the importance of the situation or context. We will always reach for a "dispositional" explanation for events, as opposed to a contextual explanation. In one experiment, for instance, a group of people are told to watch two sets of similarly talented basketball players, the first of whom are shooting baskets in a well-lighted gym and the second of whom are shooting baskets in a badly lighted gym (and obviously missing a lot of shots). Then they are asked to judge how good the players were. The players in the well-lighted gym were considered superior.[4]

This FAE tendency suggests that we most naturally focus on the person and what is right or wrong with that person rather than giving our attention to the larger picture or the issues that can help explain the behavior. We have a natural tendency to blame people rather than trying to understand the system or the context that might underlie the behavior. As Malcolm Gladwell, the journalist reporting on the FAE, concludes, "There is something in all of us that makes us instinctively want to explain the world around us in terms of people's essential attributes."[5]

While others in the congregation will turn first to blame and explanations of what is wrong with the other people in the congregation, the leader needs to remain poised and descriptive. A great deal of power rests in describing simply and accurately what occurs in the congregation as an expression of normal and normative generational behavior. To do so without attributing values of right or wrong and without diagnosing the limits or pathologies of people, the leader must exercise self-management to avoid being caught up in reflexive behavior and FAEs.

This is not to suggest that all of our congregations are free of people who act out their pathologies or engage in truly offensive behaviors. However, leaders must do the hard work of description and understanding that allows them to start from normative positions where more helpful learning can be found. One may need to conclude that the behavior witnessed is, in fact, offensive or pathological. But to start from such diagnoses is to fall prey to our own reactive limits. When others are trying to find someone to blame, leaders should step up into balcony space to find the big picture; then they should work descriptively. In this way leaders can help their congregations move to a place of learning and negotiating their differences rather than simply blaming and battling over them.

Seeking Common Space

The third principle and practice helpful to leaders is to seek common space in the congregation for people with differences instead of looking for solutions to their problems. As portrayed in the earlier description of the bimodal congregation, the search for solutions is elusive at best. Many of the issues that congregational members encounter over generational differences have no workable solution or compromise. As noted, it is not possible simultaneously to encourage and prohibit applause in a worship service. It is not possible both to spend and to save reserved funds to the satisfaction of the groups that live on either side of generational interpretation of what faithful stewardship requires.

If the leader can help others move to balcony space to capture the bigger picture of cultural influences on the congregation, and if the leader can help people, self included, to be descriptive rather than evaluative when dealing with differences, then the leader needs also to resist treating the resultant discomfort as a problem to be solved. Assuming that there is a correct answer to the problem of intergenerational discomfort quickly casts any situation into a search to distinguish right from wrong. The limit to this problem-oriented leadership strategy is that many issues that live on both sides of the cultural watershed have solutions that are right for one generation and wrong for the other. The search for solutions continually invites the dissonant voices in the congregation to compete. A search for winners and losers encourages people to engage in reflexive fight/flight behavior. Rather than focusing on the tendency of congregations to enforce "right" behaviors, leaders should refocus attention on the role of congregations in building community. As it was with the Israelites in their disorienting times of exodus and exile, the dominant question is "How do we live together when the old rules and customs have been taken from us?"

The search for common space instead of solutions can be creative, although rarely predictable. In fact, the unpredictable shifts that the congregation makes—uncontrollable by the leader—bring new promise that will outfit the congregation for its new cultural future.

Once again, let us take a look at basic systems theory. The biological research of Peter and Rosemary Grant on Daphne Major, one of the Galapagos Islands, offers insight to systems behavior by tracking the daily life of 13 species of finches found on the island. Their study offers a real-time observation of evolution. Using longitudinal data collected year after year, season after season, the Grants have observed the same finches in the evolutionary process of building new generations. Because the theory of evolution seeks to account for changes that stretch over millennia, Charles Darwin could only hypothesize an unprovable theory from brief observations made during his own travels to the Galapagos. Darwin's theory has been further tested over the years through the examination of fossil remains. But it has been only through the work of researchers such as the Grants that examples of evolutionary change have been tracked in real time by careful observation of species behavior in controlled environments such as that provided by Daphne Major. Highly supportive of Darwin's original thesis, the closer examination by the Grants suggests that species are surprisingly more collaborative than once believed. Not limited to competition to guarantee survival, the species of finches also demonstrated collaboration when the environmental system required.[6] For example, large-beaked finches seemed voluntarily to limit their feeding to large seeds during the scarcity of dry seasons, to make available the smaller seeds on which small-beaked finches depended.

More to the point is the "principle of divergence" that the Grants observed as a part of the biological system that supported the creation of new species.[7] This principle addresses, among other things, how a new species can be brought forth from established and competing species that live side by side. From the perspective of systems theory, two species of finches living side by side in their own established niches on Daphne Major are not dissimilar from the two generational value systems living side by side in their own established niches in the congregation. If competition is the only mode of coexistence, if winners and losers must be found, then in any time of scarcity in the environment, one species will overwhelm and destroy the other. One generational value system will attempt to dislodge and force the other out. If insufficient resources or opportunities are available to nourish both, competition will enforce a "solution" that eliminates the weaker or lesser partner in the system. This outcome is the result of assuming that generational discomforts are a "problem" and that multiple preferences cannot be sustained in the congregational system.

The principle of divergence, however, offers an alternative in which the development of new territory and new species can be the natural product of an assumption that the system can support more differences, not less. This principle demonstrates that as differences develop in the system, the two older neighboring species with established niches intuitively and voluntarily move apart from each other and go in search of new niches to sustain them. As they move apart, they leave behind a space in the environmental system that provides a niche to support the newly forming species. This path of divergence is provided not by minimizing the differences in the two species but by deepening and attending to the differences.

To understand this principle it is important to recognize that individual finches do not all occupy the same space within their species. Size and shape of beak are the primary distinguishing characteristics of a species. So, for example, a species of large finches with straight beaks might live side by side with a species of smaller finches with short, sharp beaks. Some finches, because of body size and beak, represent their species more precisely; some represent it to a lesser degree. Within the large-bodied, straight-beaked species, those finches that are sufficiently large with truly straight beaks best represent their species and live at the center of that species. Finches that are clearly of the same species but have smaller bodies or less-straight beaks live closer to the edge or boundaries of the species. The same propensity is found in the neighboring species of small, sharp-beaked finches. Here again the best specimens, most representative of the species, live at the center, while the birds that less clearly exhibit the markers of the species live closer to the edge.

When something new happens among the finches, it happens at the edge, not at the center where individuals best represent the species. At the edge of the area occupied by big-bodied, straight-beaked finches live those birds that have smaller bodies or less-straight beaks. At the edge of the habitat of the small, sharp-beaked finches live the birds that are a bit too big or that have elongated beaks. It is at the edges where the boundaries become permeable. The smaller of the big-bodied finches encounter the larger of the small-bodied finches. Instead of seeing only species-specific differences that would drive them back closer to their own species' center, these "edge" birds encounter a new similarity based on a commonality with the birds living on the edge of the neighboring species. They find as much similarity with the birds at the edge of the competing species as they do with the birds that live at the center of their own species.

When something new happens with the finches, it happens at the edges of the species as those edges overlap. Birds that once were part of one species begin to mate with the lesser representatives of the neighboring species, and a new species begins to take shape somewhere between the two existing species. The truly remarkable systems response comes in the principle of divergence, which suggests that when something new happens at the edge of the two established species, the original species do not ignore it. Rather they pay attention to the newly forming species because it will have new skills and abilities and will tend to prosper. Reporting on the Grants' work, author and science journalist Jonathan Weiner writes:

> The lucky individual that finds a different seed or nook, or niche will fly up and out from beneath the Sisyphean rock of

competition. It will tend to flourish and so will its descendants—
that is, those that inherit the lucky character that had set it a little
apart. Individuals that diverge from the maddening crowd will
tend to prosper, while the rest will be ground down.[8]

Marvelously as the new species magnifies its differences, the two original
species begin to shift their environmental niche and move farther apart
from one another. The center birds of the original species locate and establish new environmental niches that will sustain them. And what is left is a
new niche, available to sustain the new species that is developing in the
middle.

Human beings are not finches, and caution must be exercised when
lessons from the sciences are applied to human social systems, whether
those lessons come from popular explorations of chaos theory in the new
physics or the lessons of species development from evolutionary biology.
But humans do live in social systems that follow basic systems patterns.
And congregations are an example of such a social system.

If we look at the two generationally based cultural value systems that
live side by side in the congregation, we can observe similar systems behavior. Some individuals are so clearly representative of their cultural value
system that they live at the center of that subsystem in the congregation.
They are the product of the GI value system or of the consumer value
system, and they can be no other. These are the people who most strongly
push, in evaluative ways, the "rightness" of the behaviors of their own value
system. These individuals are most uncomfortable and complain most loudly
when they confront the differences represented by the opposing cultural
value system. And these are the members who cry most loudly for their
clergy or lay leaders to "do something" to make things right again. Making
things right again commonly means that leaders should rule in favor of their
preferences and eliminate the discomforting differences.

The insistence on viewing generational differences as a problem comes
from those who live at the centers of cultural value systems. As noted
earlier, these center folk are more clearly defined by their tenure of membership in the congregation than by age or generational location. If the pastor falls into the trap of responding to these central people with attempts to
"fix" the discomfort associated with the "new thing" happening at the edge,
the result is continued competition. Weiner's characterization of this competition as "Sisyphean" seems accurate. Trying to "solve" the problem of
competition is guaranteed to keep competition alive in the system.

However, each generationally based cultural value system in the congregation includes individuals who live close to the edge of their own value preferences and overlap with individuals who live close to the edge of the competing value system. These "edge people" understand and appreciate their own value systems and can clearly express the preferences of those systems. But not being tied only to those values, not living at the center of their value system, they can help to produce something new at the edge.

These edge people live within their own value system but demonstrate an openness to the needs of other groups. Asked to lead some balcony learning with the planning team at a large United Methodist church in the South, I first met with the group. It included a retired business executive whom I quickly identified as a GI value system representative. However, when I invited people to introduce themselves and say a word about why they wanted to be on the planning team, this man said he had asked to be put on the team. Quite pleased with his church the way it was, he had little need for the church to do anything different, he said. However, he added, he had four little grandchildren in the church, and he wanted to help his congregation get ready to meet their needs. As I watched this man work, I realized that I had found an edge person who would be invaluable in supporting the new things that could happen at the edge in this congregation.

People living at the center of their value system often see differences as a problem and push vigorously for solutions that favor their own preferences. Leaders need to stay connected to these people and listen carefully to them. But leaders need not shape the congregation's agenda to satisfy people with this problem-centered orientation.

People living at the edge of their value system are sensitive to differences and willingly learn more about them. Leaders need to help the edge people find common space and encourage them to shape their own agenda, one related to experiments in developing new congregational practices. It is common for edge people to build an agenda that does not attempt to solve the unsolvable or to eliminate all discomforts. One such group of edge people in a congregation was asked to address the complaints about the new contemporary worship service. The group quickly realized that it could not satisfactorily persuade everyone of the importance of a new worship setting. So as a true edge group, the members changed the agenda. Instead of addressing worship changes, they began to ask how the congregation could more effectively form and deepen community. They explored how to listen to complaints responsibly without giving in to subgroup pressures.

They looked for ways to stay in touch with the people most upset with the change—members who were threatening to leave the congregation. They developed relationship-deepening social events to bring people together outside worship. And they worked with their minister to develop balcony-space opportunities for members to learn more about traditions of worship.

Edge people do not depend on solutions. They need common space. Leaders need to identify these edge people and bring them together across their value-system differences in structured conversation. They respond well to balcony-space learning. Providing such opportunities across generational value-system differences gives the edge people—and the congregation—a new common language and shared ideas they can use as they search for new ways. Once again, leaders cannot control what these edge people will learn, what conclusions they will draw, what new agenda they will shape, or what actions they will pursue. But, as in every faithful spiritual pilgrimage, the leader is not responsible for where the trip ends. The leader invites people on the journey and provides them with resources along the way.

Installing Civility

Several times I have returned to the theme of generational cohorts not speaking well of each other. Since we all tend to view our own values and life lessons as correctives to the excesses or limits of what went before, and as standards insufficiently upheld by those who follow, a sense of right and wrong is often layered over how we believe others live. Particularly in a time such as our own that honors individuals, our judgments of others can carry a less-than-civil tone.

I have explored the natural incivility of the culture of individualism in my book *Behavioral Covenants in the Congregation: A Handbook for Honoring Differences.*[9] If the individual is seen as the final arbiter of what is right in his or her own life, it is difficult to insist that anyone submit to community standards or practices that acknowledge or appreciate the needs of others. I noted earlier that members of each generational cohort are sufficiently enculturated in the media and advertising shift toward pure markets that they desire both consumer goods and living conditions that fit their preferences. All of us want it our own way. And the culture helps each of us to have it our own way by separating us into our own image tribes where we feel comfortable on an island populated by similar people like us who also want it our way.

In a culture of individualism everyone is supported in the conviction of a personal right to live life on one's own terms. This cultural predisposition toward the individual lends itself to an incivility in which people openly compete with others perceived to be different without imposing limits or boundaries on their own behaviors or preferences. Recently I sat in a movie theater in front of a man whose cell phone rang midway through the movie. He unhesitatingly answered the call. In a group setting like a movie theater, where audience satisfaction depends on the individual's willingness not to talk, this man apparently had no doubt that his personal phone call took precedence over the audience's purpose of watching a movie. It was a small matter and a trivial annoyance, to be sure. But it was evidence of the extent of uncivil behavior tolerated in our culture because the individual has learned to take priority over the needs of others.

What is missing from cultural behavior that produces such uncivil practices is a sense of sacrifice. Yale law professor Stephen Carter notes that sacrificial civility has two components: "generosity when there is cost, and trust when there is risk."[10] Generosity without cost is mere politeness, and trust when there is no risk is merely the status quo. Congregations, because they are communities created to live by faith values, are meant to live beyond incivility. Congregations are communities in which generosity is to be practiced when there is cost, and trust is to be offered especially at the point of risk. Using Carter's definition of sacrificial civility, congregations are expected to be places of civility for reasons of faith, even when they find themselves in a culture of individualism that stresses competition.

Civil behavior does not come naturally in an age of individualism. It is more common for people, even members of congregations, to default to the norms of the culture: The need of the individual precedes the need of the group. Changing a long-established worship pattern is perceived in the same way that we perceive a change in the township or city tax base. The natural response in the current cultural moment is to ask whether this change is good "for me." People offer support or resistance from that perspective. If the worship change or the tax change does not meet one's own need, then one feels justified in using competitive strategies to fight the change openly. Indeed, in many congregations one would be hard-pressed to see how the competitive, even combative, behavior in a meeting about worship changes differs from behavior at the township meeting over the tax change.

Bimodal congregations are configured to produce discomfort for those who cannot have their own preferences honored. Bimodal congregations, by their internal configuration, are sacrificial communities in which generosity and trust must be offered at those points where personal costs will have to be paid to accommodate changes needed by the whole group. In the current cultural environment it should not surprise us to encounter uncivil behavior in bimodal congregations. But because congregations are faith communities, leaders need to install new standards of civility that will see the congregation through difficult times of learning and decision making.

Leaders need to set the standard for behavior in the congregation. As noted, change comes from the edge in all systems. If change comes from the edge, health comes from the center of the congregation, where leaders operate. Tensions and anxieties naturally rise within the congregation as bimodal differences are encountered. Perhaps the most significant variable in determining how helpfully or hurtfully the differences will be engaged is the response of leaders. Leaders need to remain poised, listen carefully, and behave civilly in response to the demands of others.

In healthy congregations nonreactive civil behavior by the leaders is sufficient to remind others of the community standards of the congregation, and sacrificial civility will rule the day. In these healthy congregations leaders may simply need to initiate a conversation at a board meeting or retreat to remind themselves of how to stay poised and remain civil as members react to tensions or changes that stem from their bimodal differences. In highly anxious situations or in less healthy congregations, however, civility may need to be introduced more formally by the development and use of congregational behavioral covenants (the subject of my earlier book).[11] Whether through natural reminders or intentional covenants, civility and sacrificial community must be exemplified by the leadership of the congregation, or they will not be experienced in the wider body.

Leaders live and work in the middle in bimodal congregations. The middle is not a comfortable place to be. Leaders need to listen to the natural discomfort that will be expressed in these congregations. And then, rather than rush ahead to find solutions that will make everyone happy (solutions that are elusive if not nonexistent), leaders need to help their bimodal members remain in their discomfort as the place of real learning and community building. An inability to produce answers does not indicate that leaders play a passive role in these congregations. Indeed, leaders have the larger and more difficult task of helping members learn and open themselves to the movement of God in new ways in their midst.

When the search for answers and solutions is unproductive and retards the development of the congregation, leaders can pursue other clear goals that will support the members. Moving to the balcony, working descriptively, seeking common space, and installing civility are worthy activities for leaders. Rather than treating the bimodal congregation as though it were a problem to be solved, these new activities by leaders to support learning can enable the bimodal congregation to be the transforming community it needs to be in this time of cultural change.

CHAPTER 10

Passing the Faith On

O ften when leaders of bimodal congregations call me as a consultant to help with problems in their congregation, shadings of pride or pleasure slip into the conversation. The presenting problem may center on leaders' difficulty in reaching agreement on planning goals—and concern registers in their voices. The difficulty seems to be linked to the new people who have been coming to the congregation recently—and a bit of pride can be heard.

The evidence offered by bimodal, multigenerational congregations is encouraging, but it is a mixture of problem and pride, puzzle and progress. Often uncomfortable with themselves, challenged by subtle differences in cultural life lessons and values that are difficult to articulate, these bimodal congregations are not easy to lead. However, they show healthy signs of an enduring faith that shifts and shapes itself to speak to new generations. In her work on congregations as bearers of tradition, Dorothy Bass, director of the Valparaiso Project on the Education and Formation of People in Faith, notes that changes in worship, the rearrangement of worship or program schedules, and the changes of music or liturgy prompted by a new day are not departures from tradition but rather signs that the tradition is living and vibrantly interactive with the world.[1]

Living faith traditions, like living languages, are difficult to master because they continually shift and change themselves and are subject to regional accents and intonations. My own academic encounter with languages provided ample proof of the difficulty of living traditions. I seem to possess what is known as a "tin ear" when it comes to listening critically to living, spoken, languages. In other words, I have no idea what I am hearing. I did fine with Latin and New Testament Greek, since these were "dead languages" not actively spoken today. For me, these languages could be mastered. They had limited, unchanging rules. They held still, and with some hard work I could manage them. That was not so in my encounter with Spanish—very much alive and subject to the influence of cultures and the individual twists of speakers. Studying Spanish involved a language lab, where I donned earphones and listened to a voice speaking and shaping the language. As I listened to other speakers who used the language in ways that sounded different, I realized that this language could be spoken in many ways and that it was a language for which culture mattered.

One of my most notorious language encounters—a story still enjoyed by my family—came during a visit to London, as I stepped into a taxi. The cabby simply asked where my wife and I wanted to go. "Huh?" was my informed response. He asked again, more slowly and with greater clarity. I turned to my wife and asked, "What did he say?" I had not understood one word that he uttered, and yet the driver was speaking English, my own language! His English came through a Cockney filter. The malleability of a living language, like a living faith, allows it to serve people in multiple settings. Words can come and go as some expressions become outworn and new usages are coined regionally. Continuously serving a changing culture, these living languages are marvelously creative and often difficult to master. Abundant creativity coupled with difficulty of mastery also describes living faith traditions. The very malleability that allows for a healthy encounter with a changing culture also makes the tradition and the congregation that bear the tradition more difficult to understand and lead.

To provide leadership to a congregation that is in process of change, shaping itself and its tradition for the future, leaders need to wean it from some older standards and practices. These once served the congregation well, but continued dependence upon them limits the degree to which the congregation can reshape itself for a new day. In conclusion I would point to three old standards and practices whose grip needs to be broken in many congregations to allow the health and vitality of bimodal congregations to gain freedom.

1. Axiomatic Mission Statements, Assumed Missions

Mission statements can be axiomatic or unique. The axiomatic ones describe a mission or purpose that fits not only the congregation in question, but all congregations of that faith tradition. An axiomatic mission statement essentially states that this congregation is like all other congregations of its tradition, and it does what other congregations do. Books of polity such as the *Presbyterian Book of Order* or the *Book of Discipline of the United Methodist Church* carry axiomatic descriptions of the purposes of congregations in their respective tradition. These books of polity also carry generic definitions and descriptions of the structure needed to function as a congregation, generic principles and practices, and generic standards by which to evaluate congregational practice.

In an earlier day dominated by the group norms of the GI value system, such approaches were appropriate. Generic mission statements declaring that the purpose of the congregation was to provide worship and sacraments, to develop community and provide personal care for members, to offer education to children and adults, and to serve the larger world—such statements sufficed. These statements served congregations well as they worked to be like one another within a given tradition.

However, at a time of cultural watershed when new voices are re-shaping the faith tradition to speak to a changing culture, the axiomatic understanding of mission must give way to experimentation and the unique framing of purpose and mission for each congregation. Congregations and their leaders need to wrestle directly with a unique understanding of their purpose and mission because of who they are, their location, and the age in which they live. A congregation's definition of purpose must be specific, shaped by the conditions that confront it. Members cannot assume that their mission or purpose is identical to that of other congregations, even those of the same tradition.

It is difficult to frame a unique definition of purpose that allows a specific congregation to fit within its own faith tradition while expanding its freedom to speak to a new cultural moment. To a large extent, crafting such a document depends upon spiritual discernment that allows the congregation to identify where it fits (and doesn't fit) within its own faith tradition. The connections forged with the biblical story in chapters 3, 5, and 7 are brief examples of this difficult work.

To claim the unique mission that belongs to a certain congregation with life-giving energy and clarity, leaders need to let go of formulaic and axiomatic understandings of their purpose. Old definitions and assumptions about purpose and mission need to be released so that the search may begin for new understandings to address the challenges of the new multi-generational day.

2. Evaluation Systems Built on Complaints

To move ahead in discovering the congregation's purpose and living into the new culture, leaders must help others let go of old models of evaluation that depend on complaints. Indeed, one of the most difficult tasks taken up by laypeople in a congregation is that of evaluating staff or programs. Most church members are not located at a vantage point that gives them clarity about what staff members do, or who is served by the church's programs. Most people have a fragmented perspective of their own congregation, in which they experience and therefore understand only a limited portion of what the staff and programs do and whom they serve.

Because they do not have full picture, most personnel committees or program review groups lack clear standards by which to conduct their evaluations. Put in a difficult spot of needing to evaluate but denied access to information by which to evaluate, most committees or groups "default" to the general question: "Are there any complaints?" This baseline evaluation question allows groups to assume that if no complaints surface, everything must be going well. If complaints are lodged, there must be problems to be addressed.

Healthy bimodal congregations focused on learning the new culture must give up the default system of evaluation-by-complaint. Indeed, the bimodal congregation has been described as being uncomfortable with itself because of the deep, value-centered differences that live within. That being the case, leaders need to assume that complaints will arise in the healthy bimodal congregation and that they are evidence that essential differences are being negotiated.

To move ahead, leaders in bimodal congregations need to accept the presence of complaints as normative. Grousing is not necessarily evidence that something is wrong. Those responsible for evaluating cannot easily use gripes and criticisms as the early warning system of whether things are going right or not. Indeed, the bimodal congregation's evaluation of staff and programs must be related to the much more difficult standard of clear goals set in advance for staff and program committees to follow. The appropriate evaluation question is not whether everyone is "happy" as indicated by an absence of complaints. The question that must rest at the heart of the evaluative process in bimodal congregations is whether those with responsibility for leadership or programs did what they agreed to do and whether their efforts were effective.

An oversensitivity to complaints allows critics to bring efforts at change and negotiation to a halt. If leaders continually believe that gripes are problems to be fixed, others quickly learn that efforts and experiments at change can be easily redirected or stopped by a criticism that turns attention to what is perceived as wrong.

3. Dependence on Democratic Decision Making

Finally, leaders must let go of their total dependence upon democratic decision-making processes such as *Robert's Rules of Order* and their commitment to majority-based decision making. This is not to suggest that voting has no appropriate role in the decision-making process of congregations. Indeed, when a clear decision needs to be made and the question can appropriately be framed as a choice between two alternatives, democratic practices of decision making may be helpful.

However, leadership tools of decision making such as voting and *Robert's Rules of Order* limit us to oppositional thinking: we reduce a question to a matter of which side or opinion is right and which is wrong. Moving too quickly to finding the majority preference (the effect of voting) or allowing conversation only by the rules (the strategy of *Robert's Rules*) fails to honor the negotiation of a living faith tradition that lies at the heart of the bimodal congregation. Multigenerational negotiation of the faith tradition depends upon keeping the conversation alive and healthy—an aim not always met by moving quickly to a decision, no matter how fair and "by the rules" the process may have been. Moving quickly to democratic decision-making processes may help reduce discomfort in the congregation by identifying who wins and thereby allowing the "winners" to move ahead while the "losers" adapt or leave. But the price of such instant comfort is the interruption of important negotiation and learning what the multigenerational congregation must do to live.

Indeed, democratic decision making is excellent when we need to move to action. Frequently, however, the bimodal congregation needs to move not to action but to learning. To make this shift, leaders will need to continue experiments with the process of discernment and with strategies of building consensus to make decisions. Much slower and more deliberate, these alternative forms of decision making allow for conversation with self, others, and God, and leave room for the negotiation that will inform the way in which the faith and life of the congregation are appropriately shaped. Increasingly, bimodal congregations are returning to earlier traditions in their faith histories to reclaim discernment and consensus for use in this new multigenerational context. To do so, leaders must first let go of their singular dependence on *Robert's Rules* and traditional voting procedures that have served congregations well in past generations.

Learning the Current Cultural Watershed

What future implications can be seen in the current bimodal distribution in many congregations? As I work with groups of leaders in congregations and they discover that the multigenerational bimodal model describes their own congregation, the conversation often turns to implications for the future. If the bimodal description is accurate, what will happen in the future? I would point to two insights that come from these conversations.

First, the GI-value portion of the congregation needs to stop waiting for the consumer-value portion to "grow up." Commonly leaders find that long-tenured members are impatiently waiting for the short-tenured part of the congregation to change its ways and behave like the GI cohort. In other words, the GI cohort expects that newer and younger members will eventually sign up for the vacant committee slots, vote for saving the reserved funds instead of spending them, attend the established women's circle, and support the annual holiday bazaar. This expectation rests on an assumption that the issue is one of maturity. In other words, longtime members assume that as people "grow up," they will realize what is appropriate conduct and begin to behave like members of the GI generation.

However, the cultural shift being lived out in the bimodal congregation relates not to personal maturity but to newly forming cultural values that are intended to change and compensate for older cultural values. Baby boomers, baby busters, millennials, and GenXers will not mature into GIs. They will live out their own cultural values and life lessons, to be superseded by the ideas of still younger cohorts with different life lessons, assumptions, and values.

A difficult implication of the bimodal congregation is that current leaders need to stop waiting for the congregation to return to past values and practices. Instead, we all need to move ahead with learning the new values and new cultural needs, and learn how to live together as faith communities in authentic ways.

The second insight: Leaders in a majority of congregations need to understand the great watershed cultural difference before moving on to address the reified differences. The watershed difference between the GI culture and the consumer culture is the basic shift to be negotiated in the bimodal congregation. It involves the fundamental generational markers we have identified—such as the shift from group identity to individual identity, or from deferred pleasure to instant gratification.

On the consumer-culture side of this watershed are a host of other reified generational differences. Within the consumer-value system cohorts, late boomers are different from early boomers. The busters differ from the late boomers. GenXers and millennials are different from busters and from each other. Each of these cultural subgroups has different life experiences and expectations. As we begin to pay attention to the reified differences of our generational cohorts, we become increasingly aware of the pure-market differences of additional layers of audiences that our faith traditions must still learn to address and to invite into our congregations.

In reading pure-market analyses of these newer generational cohorts such as the GenX group, many congregations want to leap ahead to plan worship and programs that will attract this new audience. However, one of the findings from bimodal congregations is that leaders need first to learn how to negotiate the more basic cultural divide between GI and consumer values. To jump ahead and first do GenX pure-market ministry may throw the whole congregation into conflict. An exception is the largest congregations, where it is possible to do GI and GenX ministries simultaneously because these two very different groups do not need to live with and encounter each other so directly in the large congregation.

However, the hope and the experience of bimodal congregations is that once the great divide between the GI and consumer value systems is learned (and appreciated), it is much easier to move on to negotiate the differences that will come with succeeding generational cohorts. As we learn to hold our faith traditions and our congregations more lightly so that they can live in more adaptive and malleable ways, successive transitions to new generational cohorts may be easier to negotiate.

In chapter 3, I noted biblical theologian Walter Brueggemann's suggestion that the Old Testament exile was perhaps the most accurate metaphor for the current situation of the North American congregation. That being so, we must remind ourselves constantly that the time of exile is never comfortable but always productive. As the old world with its known rules and expectations is torn away, those in exile must learn new rules and expectations. New standards of community must be discovered; new agreements and practices of the faith must be developed. In exile these agreements and practices develop as people discuss what they miss from the old and what they need to create for the new. The exile that comes as we are moved from one cultural reality and thrust into a new one can be managed only as leaders help people let go of the old so that they may take hold of the new.

Leaders are tempted to take culturally exiled people back into a comfort zone that was lost when they left the dominant culture behind, or to thrust the people into the new without preparation. The more appropriate task of leaders is to hold people responsible in the conversation of the present moment. The bimodal congregation has much to teach us. As faith communities facing new cultural realities, we have much to learn. There is no better time to be a participant in a congregation than when God is doing a new thing.

Introduction

1. Sidney Schwarz, "Transforming Synagogues," *Sh'ma*, 30, no. 564 (September 1999): 5.

2. For example, Gil Rendle, *Leading Change in the Congregation: Spiritual and Organizational Tools for Leaders* (Bethesda: Alban Institute, 1998), 77-103.

3. Dorothy Bass, "Congregations and the Bearing of Traditions," *American Congregations*, vol. 2, ed. James P. Wind and James W. Lewis (Chicago: University of Chicago Press, 1994), 172.

4. Loren Mead, *The Once and Future Church: Reinventing the Congregation for a New Mission Frontier* (Washington, D.C.: Alban Institute, 1991), 85.

5. William Bridges, *Managing Transitions: Making the Most of Change* (Reading, Mass.: Addison-Wesley, 1991), 34.

6. William Strauss and Neil Howe, *The Fourth Turning: An American Prophecy* (New York: Broadway Books, 1997), 40, 78.

Chapter 1

1. Craig Kennet Miller, *Post Moderns: The Beliefs, Hopes, and Fears of Young Americans* (Nashville: [United Methodist] Discipleship Resources, 1996).

2. Leonard Sweet, "The Back Page," *Homiletics* (January-March 1996): 60.

3. Richard H. Gentzler, Jr., and Carolyn S. Poole, *The Pulse of United Methodist Baby Boomers* (Nashville: General Board of Discipleship, United Methodist Church, 2000).

4. Bill Easum, "Worship in a Changing Culture," *Contemporary Worship*, ed. Tim and Jan Wright (Nashville: Abingdon, 1997).

5. Joseph Turrow, *Breaking Up America: Advertisers and the New Media World* (Chicago: University of Chicago Press, 1997).

6. Turrow, *Breaking Up America,* ix.

7. *Associate Manual* (Costa Mesa, Calif.: Church Information and Development Services, 1990), 47.

8. Marc Fisher, "Adding Up the Radio Countdown," *Washington Post* (2 December 1997): sec. B, p. 1.

9. Turrow, *Breaking Up America,* 4.

10. Turrow, *Breaking Up America,* 5, 106.

11. Turrow, *Breaking Up America,* 3.

12. Turrow, *Breaking Up America,*126.

13. Stephen Carter, *Civility: Manners, Morals, and the Etiquette of Democracy* (New York: Basic Books, 1998), 170.

14. Ian Evison, Worship Workshop, Indianapolis Center for Congregations, 19 January 2001.

15. Gil Rendle, "On Not Fixing the Church," *Congregations* (May-June 1997): 15-17, and "Unhooking the System," *Congregations* (July-August 1997): 14-16.

16. Gregory Bateson, *Steps to an Ecology of Mind* (New York: Ballantine Books, 1972), 208.

17. Mark Chaves, *How Do We Worship?* (Bethesda: Alban Institute, 1999), 7-8.

18. www.alban.org/NCS.asp

19. Norman Shawchuck, Philip Kottler, Bruce Wrenn, and Gustave Rath, *Marketing for Congregations: Choosing to Serve People More Effectively* (Nashville: Abingdon, 1992), 104.

Chapter 2

1. C. Kirk Hadaway and David A. Roozen, *Rerouting the Protestant Mainstream: Sources of Growth and Opportunities for Change* (Nashville: Abingdon, 1995), 47.

2. Wade Clark Roof, *A Generation of Seekers: The Spiritual Journeys of the Baby Boom Generation* (San Francisco: HarperSanFrancisco, 1994), 54-60.

3. Strauss and Howe, *The Fourth Turning,* 65.

4. Roof, *Generation of Seekers,* 3.

5. Diana L. Eck, *A New Religious America* (San Francisco: HarperSanFrancisco, 2001), 61.

6. Lawrence A. Hoffman, *From Ethnic to Spiritual: A Tale of Four Generations* (n.c.: Synagogue 2000 Library, 1996), 3.

7. Roger Fisher and William Ury, *Getting to Yes: Negotiating Agreement Without Giving In* (New York: Penguin Books, 1981).

8. Speed Leas, *Discover Your Conflict Management Style* (Bethesda: Alban Institute, 1997), 24.

9. Jackson W. Carroll, "Bridging Worlds: The Generational Challenge to Congregational Life," *Circuit Rider* 22:5 (September-October 1999): 23.

10. For example, Episcopal Church statisticians noted that despite the church's decline in membership, average attendance increased by 31 percent between 1974 and 1998, measured by averaging the attendance at "four key Sundays" during the year. This increase was in contrast to the 25 percent increase in the general population during the same period (Zacchaeus Project Report, June 1999, 57). Similarly the United Methodist Church reported six consecutive years of U.S. attendance increases and noted that in 1998 the average Sunday attendance increased by 13,000, or 0.37 percent. ([United Methodist] *Newscope* 27:48 [26 November 1999]).

Chapter 3

1. Richard Lischer, *Open Secrets: A Spiritual Journey Through A Country Church* (New York: Doubleday, 2001), 237-238.

2. Walter Brueggemann, "Preaching Among Exiles," *Circuit Rider* 22:4 (July-August 1999): 22.

Chapter 4

1. Daniel Yankelovich, *New Rules: Searching for Self-Fulfillment in a World Turned Upside Down* (New York: Bantam Books, 1982), 6.

2. William Strauss and Neil Howe, *Generations: The History of America's Future, 1584 to 2069* (New York: Quill–William Morrow, 1991), 264-265.

3. Robert Wuthnow, "Returning to Practice," *IONS Noetic Sciences Review*, (August-November 1999): 34.

4. Wuthnow, "Returning to Practice," 34.

5. Yankelovich, *New Rules,* 227.

6. Gil Rendle, "Living Into the New World" video, (Bethesda: Alban Institute, 2000). To order, call (800) 486-1318.

Chapter 8
1. The Holy Bible, RSV (Oxford, England: Oxford University Press, 1962), 1390.
2. Susan A. Wheelan, *Group Process: A Developmental Approach* (Boston: Allyn & Bacon,1994), 38-39.
3. Wheelan, *Group Process,* 126.
4. Myron Magnet, *The Dream and the Nightmare: The Sixty's Legacy to the Underclass* (San Francisco: Encounter Books, 1993), 29.
5. Alex Ayres, ed., *The Wit and Wisdom of Mark Twain* (New York: Harper & Row, 1987), 255.
6. Richard D. Thau and Jay S. Heflin, eds., *Generations Apart: Xers vs. Boomers vs. the Elderly* (New York: Prometheus Books,1997), 17.
7. Thau and Heflin, eds., *Generations Apart,* 81f.
8. Strauss and Howe, *Generations,* 350.
9. Strauss and Howe, *The Fourth Turning,* 88.
10. Tom Brokaw, *The Greatest Generation* (New York: Random House, 1998).
11. Tom Freston, National Press Club Luncheon, Washington, D.C. (3 March 1997).

Chapter 9
1. Ronald Heifetz and David Laurie, "The Work of Leadership," *Harvard Business Review* (January-February 1997).
2. Peter Steinke, *How Your Church Family Works: Understanding Congregations as Emotional Systems* (Bethesda: Alban Institute, 1993), 14-18.
3. Roberta M. Gilbert, *Extraordinary Relationships: A New Way of Thinking About Human Interactions* (New York: John Wiley & Sons, 1992), 39.
4. Malcolm Gladwell, *The Tipping Point: How Little Things Can Make a Big Difference* (New York: Little, Brown, 2000), 160.
5. Gladwell, *Tipping Point,* 161.
6. Jonathan Weiner, *The Beak of the Finch* (New York: Vintage, 1994), 56-60.
7. Weiner, *Beak of the Finch,* 140-142.
8. Weiner, *Beak of the Finch,* 142.
9. Gil Rendle, *Behavioral Covenants In the Congregation: A Handbook for Honoring Differences* (Bethesda: Alban Institute, 2000).

10. Carter, *Civility,* 92.

11. Rendle, *Behavioral Covenants*

Chapter 10

1. Bass, "Congregations and the Bearing of Traditions," 172.

Following are a number of suggestions for leaders who would like to understand more about the bimodal, multigenerational congregation and the cultural context in which these congregations live. Included in this brief list are a number of resources that can be used with others to learn more about your own congregation.

- *Balcony "Big Picture" videos from the Alban Institute. Videos are excellent tools to use at leadership retreats, board meetings, or other learning moments to share "big picture" ideas with leaders. Videos present ideas in a short period of time and give leaders a shared language to describe and work with their own situation.*

  ❑ Mead, Loren. *The Once and Future Church Collection.* Bethesda: Alban Institute, 2001.
  ❑ Rendle, Gil. *Living Into the New World* video. Bethesda: Alban Institute, 2001.

- Further reading to deepen personal understanding or to engage others in learning:

  ❑ Generational value systems: Strauss, William, and Neil Howe. *The Fourth Turning: An American Prophecy.* New York: Broadway Books, 1997.
  ❑ The cultural impact of advertising, media, and the segmentation of the American community into separate image tribes: Turrow, Joseph. *Breaking Up America: Advertisers and The New Media World.* Chicago: University of Chicago Press, 1997.

❑ The role and importance of congregations in contemporary North
    American culture: Wind, James P., and James W. Lewis, eds. *Ameri-
    can Congregations*, vol.. 2. Chicago: University of Chicago Press,
    1997.
❑ Addressing the incivility and difficult behavior that often accom-
    pany multigenerational differences in congregations: Rendle, Gil.
    *Behavioral Covenants in Congregations: A Handbook for
    Honoring Differences*. Bethesda: Alban Institute, 2000.
❑ Understanding your own personal response and reaction to the ten-
    sion that is natural in bimodal, multigenerational congregations: Leas,
    Speed. *Discover Your Conflict Management Style*. Bethesda:
    Alban Institute, 1997.
❑ Understanding more about negotiating differences in the bimodal,
    multigenerational congregation: Fisher, Roger, and William Ury,
    Getting to Yes: Negotiating Agreement Without Giving In. New
    York: Penguin Books, 1981.